Communication

Communication

How to Connect with Anyone

Gill Hasson

CAPSTONE
A Wiley Brand

This edition first published 2019.

Registered Office
John Wiley & Sons Ltd, The Atrium, Southern Gate, Chichester, West Sussex, PO19 8SQ, United Kingdom

For details of our global editorial offices, for customer services and for information about how to apply for permission to reuse the copyright material in this book please see our website at www.wiley.com.

Library of Congress Cataloging-in-Publication Data is Available

ISBN 9780857087508 (paperback)
ISBN 9780857087430 (ePDF)
ISBN 9780857087539 (ePub)

Cover Design: Wiley
Cover Image: © madtom/Shutterstock

Set in 12/15pt SabonLTStd by SPi Gobal, Chennai, India

Printed in Great Britain by TJ International Ltd, Padstow, Cornwall, UK

10   9   8   7   6   5   4   3   2   1

To Dan with love from Mum:

*'Carpe diem. Seize the day, boys. Make your
lives extraordinary'.*

Dead Poets Society

Contents

Introduction

In 2017, Glenda and Raphi Savitz moved to Newton, Massachusetts with their 2-year-old daughter Samantha, who was born deaf. When they were out in the community, local people noticed that Glenda and Raphi were signing to Samantha. Some of them decided they wanted to learn how to communicate with Samantha too, so 20 neighbours and friends got together and hired a teacher to run a weekly evening class and teach them American Sign Language. Samantha's Mum, Glenda, told a journalist: 'Samantha's whole personality changes when she meets someone she can communicate with.'

Human beings are social beings. It's inherent in us to want to communicate and connect with each other.

We're born with an innate ability to communicate. We learn to communicate by listening to and/or watching other people; practising and then adjusting how and what we communicate according to the response we receive. We learn that there are basic rules of communication, known as the rules of reciprocal communication.

This means that we have to take turns to talk and that we need to wait until the other person has finished talking before we say something. We learn, too, that the second person to say something should respond to what the first person has said, rather than introduce a completely new subject.

Is it really that simple? Of course not. Why? Because communication is not a straightforward process, it's a dynamic process, influenced by all the complexities and uncertainties of human behaviour. Even with the most simple of communications, both people may *think* they understand what's passed between them, but often, what's occurred is a miscommunication.

Chapter 1 of this book identifies some of the issues that contribute to miscommunication; it describes how cultural, generational, and individual differences in how we communicate often lead to misunderstandings.

It's not just what we say, but what we hear, or what we *think* we hear that also leads to misunderstandings. Our assumptions, beliefs, judgements, and emotional states are often behind much of what we misconstrue and misinterpret. They can easily distort what the other person is saying.

So, although our ability to communicate is innate, we're not always that good at it! However, as well as being innate, communication is also a skill; it's an ability that we can learn to develop and improve.

In this book, the emphasis is on assertive communication. Assertive communication encourages each person to take part in a shared process; one that helps promote a genuine connection between people; a connection that involves respect and trust, confidence and empathy between people. Chapter 2 – 'What to Say and How to Say it' – describes assertive communication. It emphasizes the need to be clear and direct when you're talking to someone else; to do it in a way that makes it easy for them to listen and to understand what you mean.

Whether you're explaining your ideas, giving your opinion, giving directions, encouraging or persuading someone else, their perspective or knowledge concerning what you're talking about might be different from yours. What do they already know or not know? What might they feel about what you're talking about? Is this a good time and place for them to listen to what you have to say?

You need to be prepared to adapt the way you communicate; to be aware that *how* you say something can help make it easy for other people to listen and to understand what you mean. In Chapter 2, and in other chapters, there's advice on talking and listening to someone who has communication difficulties and you'll read that the advice for talking and listening to someone with communication difficulties can be followed by all of us, whoever we're talking or listening to.

Just as you do when you're talking to someone, when you put something in writing you need to make it easy for the other person – the reader – to understand you. When you're talking with another person – in person or on the phone – you can get an immediate response and if there are any obvious misunderstandings you're able to clarify, there and then, what you mean. But when you communicate in writing this doesn't necessarily happen, so you need to be even more sure to make your meaning clear. Chapter 3 explains how you can do this. And, as a bonus, once you've developed the ability to write more effectively, you'll find that what and how you say things also improves.

Chapter 4 is about listening. Dolly Parton once said 'It takes an awful lot of work to look this cheap.' The same is true for listening; it takes a lot of work to do something that appears to take no effort.

The way to become an effective listener is to learn and practise what's known as 'active listening'. And that requires some work on your part. But it's *always* worth it. Active listening makes communication easier and helps you better connect with others. Amongst other things, active listening enables you to concentrate on what the other person is saying and avoid interrupting. It helps you overcome your assumptions and increase your understanding; develop empathy and rapport; consider different points of view and be clear about where you do and don't agree.

But it's not just what a person says – what a person *doesn't* say – their non-verbal communication – can tell you a lot too. A person's non-verbal messages can emphasize and support what they're saying but they can also *contradict* what they're saying. Chapter 5 explains how you can better understand where a person is coming from; how you can read between the lines. You'll learn that you can't rely on a *single* gesture, facial expression, and so on to confirm what someone does or doesn't mean or what they're feeling; you'll need to take a *combination* of non-verbal signals into consideration.

This book is in two parts – Part One is concerned with the principles of effective communication. It describes what gets in the way of effective communication and it explains how, when you're talking to someone else, you can do it in a way that makes it easy for them to listen and to understand what you mean. Part One also teaches you ways to better understand what other people say and mean.

Part Two of this book shows you how these principles of good communication can be put into practice and help you better connect with others.

Whether it's just a minute waiting for an elevator with a colleague or a few hours sat next to a friend's cousin at a wedding, with some people you feel comfortable talking to them and conversation just seems to flow quite naturally. But with others, it's not so easy; trying to engage the other person is like wading through wet concrete; it's hard work. What to say? What to ask? How to respond? What if there's an awkward silence?

Chapter 6 answers all these questions. You'll learn how, in social situations, you can be more confident making small talk and how you can turn small talk into a more meaningful conversation.

If you're open, friendly, and show an interest in other people, they'll most likely want to talk with you and you'll want to talk back; to exchange ideas, thoughts and opinions, anecdotes and stories. How, though, do you respond when someone is sad and upset, distressed and struggling to cope? What to say when a family member, a friend, colleague, or your partner tells you that they're desperately unhappy and want to quit their job. Or that they're very worried about their financial situation. How to respond to a colleague who tells you that his wife has left him? Or that they or a close family member has been diagnosed with a serious illness? Chapter 7 has some clear, sound advice about what to say and how to respond to someone who's facing a difficult, challenging situation.

No doubt, like all of us, you often interact with people who have different opinions, beliefs, feelings, and needs to you. Your ability to exchange opinions feelings etc with other people, understand their perspectives, and solve problems between you will depend on how effectively you are able to communicate. Whether you're hoping to persuade others to give you something you want or do things your way, or to help you with something, accept your suggestion, or agree with your point of view, so often things don't turn out as you would like. Persuading is a skill. There are better and worse ways of doing it. Chapter 8 explains how.

In a range of situations, knowing that you have good communication skills enables you to connect more easily and feel more confident about communicating with a diverse range of people. Good communication skills help you develop friendships and relationships at work and at home.

Being able to communicate more effectively with family and friends means that you will know what to say to get others to open up to you; you will be more able to understand their feelings and emotions, what they mean and what they need. In turn, you will more likely be listened to and understood.

Being able to communicate well at work and in professional settings gets you ahead. If you're an effective communicator you can easily explain useful and interesting ideas and meet other people's responses, whatever they are. Others will take you seriously. They'll listen to what you have to say and be more likely to want to engage in discussion. You'll minimize misunderstandings and confusion and save time because others can understand information and direction you're giving them, easily and quickly.

Last but not least, in any situation, your good communication skills also enable others to communicate more clearly.

Convinced? Now you just need to know how to get those all-important skills.

Read on!

Part 1
Communicate

1
Understanding Communication and Miscommunication

The single biggest problem in communication is the illusion that it has taken place.

George Bernard Shaw

Even with the most simple of communications – one person says something to another, the other person replies – both people may *think* they understand what's passed between them, but often communication has not occurred. Instead, what has occurred is a miscommunication – the meaning has not been understood as the speaker intended it to be.

Take these exchanges between a Mum and Dad and their two young children. Dad is making breakfast. Mum is in the shower.

Dad: Josh, go and ask Mummy if she wants an egg.
Josh: OK! (runs to bathroom. Runs back to kitchen). She said YES! (Runs out of kitchen again)

Dad: Really?

Mum doesn't usually want eggs so Dad asks Ben

Dad: Ben, just go and check with Mummy; ask her if she wants an egg.

Ben: But I want an egg!

Dad: Sure. But please go and ask Mummy.

Ben: OK! (runs off. Runs back) Mummy said yes!

Dad goes to the fridge. There are only 2 eggs. He goes to the bathroom.

Dad: Sorry, after all that, you can't have an egg. We don't have enough.

Mum: (from in the shower): I don't want an egg.

Dad: What? Josh said you said 'Yes' you wanted an egg.

Mum: No, Josh knocked and said, 'Can I come in?' and I said 'Yes!'

Dad: And what about Ben? *He* said you wanted an egg.

Mum: Uh uh. Ben came in and asked if he could have an egg and I said, 'Yes, you can!'

How often do you assume someone knows what you meant but it turns out that they didn't? Recently, I was listening to a music station when I heard someone by the name of Mark phone in with a record request. His voice sounded like the friend of a friend. The next morning I texted my friend Karen to ask if it was her friend that I'd heard on the radio the previous day. She texted Mark to ask him and Mark then texted me. His text read 'Karen said you heard me on the radio. Is it true?!!' That confused me. Surely he'd know if he'd been talking on the radio? After a minute I realized what had happened.

Mark is a musician. He thought I meant I'd heard his *music* playing on the radio.

Of course, tales of miscommunication are often amusing. But just as often, they're not. A misread policy or contract, for example, a misinterpreted instruction, a misunderstanding about when and where to meet can lead to all sorts of difficulties. So can a misconstrued attempt to persuade someone to do something or an ill-timed comment about someone's efforts to achieve something.

Presumably though – unless they have malicious intent – no one sets out to miscommunicate. Likewise, no one sets out to deliberately misunderstand either. Humans are social beings; we're wired to communicate and to connect with each other; to seek out and exchange thoughts, ideas, opinions and theories, feelings and emotions, wants and needs, likes and dislikes. We want to communicate and connect with each other. So why do communications often go wrong and turn into miscommunications? Because communication isn't always a simple, straightforward process, it's a dynamic process, influenced by all the complexities and differences in human behaviour.

Often, we believe that there's a right and wrong way that we should communicate with each other. Most of the time, we are completely unaware of how our expectations and assumptions can create all sorts of communication breakdowns, misunderstandings, conflict, and distrust.

Cultural Differences

For a start, each culture has its own ideas and beliefs about what are and are not appropriate ways to communicate. There are, for example, 'rules' about eye contact or how close you can stand next to another person when you're talking with them. In some cultures, eye contact should be sporadic and people should stand at least three feet apart. In other cultures, eye contact may be considered disrespectful but it is acceptable for there to be just a short space between you when you're talking with each other.

For some cultures, it's important and considered correct to talk *indirectly* about an issue. For example, Japanese communication style is indirect and far less verbose – less wordy – than what many of us in the UK are used to. Japanese culture relies less on words to convey context; it's more focused on the posture, expression, and tone of voice of the speaker to draw meaning from what a person is saying. In order to maintain harmony throughout conversation and prevent a loss of face for either person, a Japanese person may use ambiguous speech and understatements to convey their message in a more subtle way.

The French style of communication is more direct. One reason for this is that the French language is quite precise and therefore it's difficult *not* to be direct when using it. The standard speaking style in Spanish is also more direct than English. 'Give me the key' sounds rude in English without a 'please' accompanying it, but in Spanish 'dame la llave' is perfectly acceptable.

Different cultures differ in the extent to which they communicate feelings and emotions. Some are generally open about their emotions, with hugs and kisses alternating between angry shouting and gesturing. They laugh and cry and are not afraid to show their anger, fear, frustration, and other feelings. Other cultures strive to keep their emotions hidden and believe in communicating only the factual, objective aspects of a situation. This can cause problems when people from different cultures communicate. A person from one culture may think another is out of control as they freely express their emotions. On the other hand, someone from a culture that openly expresses its emotions and feelings might consider the person from the more restrained culture as uptight.

If the people involved are not aware of the potential for such cultural misunderstandings, they are even more likely to fall victim to them!

> We're all islands shouting lies to each other across seas of misunderstanding.
>
> Rudyard Kipling

As well as differences in ways of communicating between people from different cultures and countries, different generations also have differences in their ways of communicating. I recently heard a middle-aged woman describing how irritated she was with her much younger colleagues who rarely returned her phone calls by phone. Instead they typically would text or email back a response. 'They need to stop emailing and pick up the %^$# phone!' she said.

Each generation has its own expectations about what's an appropriate way to communicate and they often communicate in different ways. When it comes to communication technology, in general, the older generations prefer talking face-to-face or on the phone, and the younger generations tend toward text-based messages like email and instant message. So, it can be very frustrating when you communicate with someone in a mode that they don't use or like; these differences in communication often create tension and lead to misunderstandings.

Individual Communication Styles

But it's not just cultural and generational differences that can occur and create problems with communication. We each have our own individual way of communicating. Think of any two people you know – two people in your family or two friends or colleagues. What sort of words do they use? How do they differ in the gestures they use? What tone of voice do they normally use? How loud or softly do they each talk? Some people love to talk! But they tend to over-explain; they find it impossible to be concise; they're long winded, giving unnecessary details. In contrast, someone else you know may be too brief and not explain things fully, leaving you to fill in the gaps and guess what they mean, or to ask questions and clarify what they're saying.

Some people are outgoing and direct communicators, others are more introverted. Generally speaking, when it comes to the way we communicate, we're all somewhere on an introvert/extrovert continuum. At one end of the continuum are 'active' communicators. Active communicators communicate in a lively, spontaneous, opportunistic way. They are direct and straightforward; they get to the point quickly and keep things moving and get things summed up. They use language that makes an impact, they're not afraid to use strong language, and are prone to exaggerate and use large gestures and animated facial expressions. They like to participate in conversation, discussion, and debates; they're not patient listeners unless they're amused or fascinated by what the other person is saying. Whether they're experts in what's being discussed or not, they come across confidently and persuasively.

Also towards the extrovert end of the communication continuum are 'purposeful' communicators. Purposeful communicators like to be clear about the aim of a conversation and to stay on track. They like ideas and issues to be discussed in a logical order. They don't like interruptions. They're not keen on chat and small talk but would rather communicate with others in a way that will get things done. Purposeful communicators use 'proper' language and don't like to hear or use slang and jargon. They may often use words to emphasize what they mean – extreme or absolute terms like 'always', 'never', 'must', 'should', or 'can't'. And they may come across as impatient and controlling.

At the more introverted end of the continuum are the 'connectors'. Connectors tend to listen more than talk – they like to 'read between the lines' and work out the feelings and intentions behind what another person is saying. They like to talk about relationships and people. They're interested in values and beliefs. They're tactful and considerate; thinking about how to phrase something so that it doesn't offend the other person. They dislike conversations that lead to conflict. Connectors like to take time to relate to and connect with others. They're friendly and approachable and welcome conversation with others. They show empathy and appreciation and communicate in a way that will promote cooperation and harmony. Connectors are good listeners, speak from the heart, are influenced by their feelings and emotions, and use their intuition. They tend to be subjective (unlike theorists who are objective).

'Theorists' are also towards the introverted end of the communication style continuum. They tend to think and deliberate during a conversation. They like to review what they've just heard and respond carefully in a way that most accurately expresses their thoughts on the matter. Their aim is to get information that will help them solve or discover something or provide new knowledge. They like talking about theories, ideas, and information rather than feelings and relationships and use wording such as 'I think' rather than 'I feel'. They'd rather say nothing than say something wrong. Unlike 'connectors', they usually avoid emotional bonding and go straight for the facts. This approach can come across as quite cold and can be off-putting to those seeking to first establish a personal connection. Theorists' body language is usually quite controlled and so may be hard for others to read. Their conversations like to take in and develop new ideas and possibilities. They enjoy describing all aspects and details of a situation or an idea. Theorists are quick to pull together odd bits of information into rational arguments.

Of course, these descriptions of the ways we communicate are general descriptions; we don't all neatly fall into one of these cultural, generational, or extroverted/introverted communication styles. None the less they serve to illustrate the fact that we don't all communicate in the same ways. And differences in the way we each communicate can present barriers that get in the way of effective communication.

What's in a Word?

> Words are the source of misunderstandings.
> Antoine de Saint-Exupéry

As well as our own particular characteristic way of communicating, the specific words we use can mean different things to different people. If, for example, a parent asks their child if their room is clean and tidy, do the parent and the child have the same definition of the words 'clean' and 'tidy'? Not likely!

Any one word may have two distinct meanings. The first meaning – the denotative meaning – refers to the definition you would find in a dictionary. The second type of meaning is the connotative meaning. The connotative meaning of a word is what the word suggests and represents to a person; the collection of ideas that they associate with that word. So, just as words like 'clean' and 'tidy' have different connotative meanings, so do words like 'Socialist' and 'Tory', 'Religion' and 'Feminist'. They each have meanings that provoke different reactions from different people.

As Dale Carnegie, author of the book *How to Make Friends and Influence People*, says, 'When dealing with people, let us remember we are not dealing with creatures of logic. We are dealing with creatures of emotion, creatures bristling with prejudices and motivated by pride and vanity.'

Gobbledygook, Gibberish, Twaddle, and Drivel

Some words have different meanings to different people, but other words can mean something to one person but mean absolutely nothing to another person. Recently, my Mum's doctor told her she might need a hip replacement but that the referral system has changed. 'I'm no longer the gatekeeper,' he said. 'It's a different pathway. I'll refer you to the physio and if they think you might need a hip replacement, the physio, not me, refers you to a consultant. It's a new pathway.' Pathway? Gatekeeper?

My Mum had no idea what he meant. (Fortunately I did and was able to explain it to her.)

Since 1979, the Plain English Campaign have been campaigning against gobbledygook, jargon, and misleading public information. On their website – www.plain english.co.uk – they have some good examples of meaningless, empty phrases. Here's a few of them. The first two are from interviews with footballers. The second two are from business managers.

- The pundits have written us off since day one but we ran the lines well and the killer pass and finish came at the right time and we'll try and use that as a springboard and push on.
- Our crosses never looked like beating the first man but he's put it right down the corridor of uncertainty at the right moment there and it's not good-night Vienna just yet.
- Our exploratory research points to compatible organizational projections.
- We need a more blue-sky approach to responsive policy consulting.

Confused? Unfortunately, Google Translate won't help; it can't make any sense of these statements either!

Assumptions and Judgements

What else gets in the way of clear communication? Not just what we say, but what we hear. Or rather, what we think we hear. Listening looks simple but it's not easy. As the Spanish saying goes 'cada cabeza es un mundo', which translates as 'every head is a world', meaning we each have our own perspective.

Our individual assumptions, beliefs, and judgements are often behind much of what we misconstrue and misinterpret. Those assumptions, beliefs and judgements, biases and prejudices can easily distort what the other person is saying to you.

For example, Tamwar was telling his friend Suzy about his colleague Sam. Suzy already knew that Sam belongs to a particular religious group and she has a view of the 'kind of people' that belong to that group. Her assumptions distorted what Tamwar was telling her. She missed the point of what Tamwar was saying about Sam, which, actually, was nothing to do with Sam's religious beliefs.

In another example, Ned, a manager, is talking with Nadia, a clerical worker, about a proposal the team has for a new project. Nadia makes some comments but Ned listens to her as 'just an admin worker' and fails to hear the insightful observation and suggestion she makes.

Too often, instead of responding to what people are actually saying and what they mean, we engage and respond to what we think they're saying and mean. It's easy to jump to conclusions and assume, for example, that the person you're listening to is always the same. For example, Dan expects that most of what Bill says will, as is usual for Bill, come from a place of self-pity. Bill is talking about his wife who he's separated from. 'She's left me, but she keeps "returning" in little ways. She wants to meet up to discuss, what seem to me, minor issues. I don't know what's going on or what to think.' Unfortunately, rather than recognize that Bill is simply confused because his wife seems to have left him, and yet, not left him, all Dan can hear is Bill feeling sorry for himself.

It's not difficult to fall into the trap of judgmental listening; to listen in order to determine whether what the other person is saying is right or wrong. Bob, for example, tells his daughter Tanya that, when he goes to the hospital, 'I want a doctor who speaks English'. Tanya immediately assumes her Dad's reasons for this are racist. And they might be. But assuming that they are only ensures a disconnect and a growing distance between them.

When Emotions Get in the Way

> Between what is said and not meant, and what is meant and not said, most of love is lost.
>
> Khalil Gibran

Our emotional reactions often play a part in how we each communicate in particular situations. Feeling frustrated, frightened, or angry can hinder communication and create misunderstandings. So can feeling stressed, intimidated, or upset.

At times like this, we resort to all kinds of inappropriate and unhelpful ways of communicating. When we're stressed, we might express our thoughts and opinions in aggressive ways; ways that are rude, mean, or abusive, and blame or even threaten other people. In contrast, when we feel unsure or intimidated we might remain passive and hold back from saying what we think or feel.

Sometimes, when we're annoyed or upset, we do and say nothing at all, but at other times we might resort to passive aggressive communication. Rather than say what we feel or think, we mutter our dissent to ourselves or use a non-verbal way of expressing our feelings, rolling our eyes or giving the other person 'dirty looks'. Passive aggressive communication is not easy to respond to because it's expressed in obscure, underhanded ways. The person communicating their resistance towards someone else does so indirectly; for example, using sarcasm or veiled hostile joking and teasing – so-called 'banter'. For whatever reason, they feel unable to say directly what they really think, feel, or want. They don't reveal what they really mean which leaves the rest of us confused as we try to work out what's going on.

So, as you can see, often communication is not straightforward. It's a dynamic process, influenced by all the complications, strengths, and limitations of human interests and behaviour. Although our ability to communicate is innate, there's all sorts of ways that communication can go wrong. But, as well as being innate, communication is also a skill; it's an ability that can be developed and improved.

In a nutshell

- Even with the most simple of communications, both people may think they understand what's passed between them, but often communication has not occurred. Instead, what has occurred is a miscommunication.
- As well as differences in ways of communicating between people from different cultures and countries, different generations also differ in how they communicate.
- We each also have our own individual style of communicating. Some people are outgoing and direct communicators, others are more reserved and introverted.
- These cultural, generational, and individual differences in communication often create tension and lead to misunderstandings.
- The specific words we use can mean different things to different people. And some words can mean something to one person but mean absolutely nothing to another person.
- It's not just what we say, but what we think we hear. Our individual assumptions, beliefs, and judgements are often behind much of what we misconstrue and misinterpret. They can easily distort what the other person is saying.

- Our emotional reactions – feeling stressed or upset in some way – can hinder communication and create misunderstandings.
- Although our ability to communicate is innate, it's also a skill; it's an ability that can be learned, developed, and improved.

2
Knowing What to Say and How to Say it

March Hare: Then you should say what you mean.

Alice: I do, at least – at least I mean what I say – that's the same thing, you know.

Mad Hatter: Not the same thing a bit! You might just as well say that 'I see what I eat' is the same thing as 'I eat what I see'!

Alice's Adventures in Wonderland. By Lewis Carroll

What the March Hare says is good advice; you should say what you mean. Whether you're telling someone what you do or don't want, what you think or how you feel, or you're explaining how to do something, making a complaint, or making small talk at a party, there's one rule: say what you mean. Do it in a way that makes it easy for other people to listen and to understand what you mean.

Mostly, we do mean exactly what we say: 'Pass the salt please.' But sometimes what we say isn't what we're really asking: 'Is there any salt?' ('Yes, there is.') In this example, hinting and implying just hides the meaning of what the person really wants. It's an indirect way of saying what you mean. So is sarcasm 'Oh! You remembered to put the salt on the table this time. Well done.'

The best way to make it easy for others to listen and understand is to be clear and direct. If you're not clear and you don't use the right words, it's all too easy for the other person to misinterpret what you said and sometimes, they'll take advantage of your ambiguity and misunderstand deliberately. For example, tell a teenager 'I want you to tidy your room' and they will tidy it in the way *they* define as tidy. In contrast, if you say exactly what you mean you're more likely to get what you want. 'I want you to tidy your room. This means picking up the clothes and books from the floor and putting them away. Bring the dirty cups and plates down to the kitchen and put them in the dishwasher. And make sure you vacuum the carpet please.'

Hit the Headline

When you've got something to tell someone, something to ask for, explain, or discuss, hit the headline first. Think about what the main point is that you need to make. You should be able to say it in one sentence. Two at the most. Then elaborate, following the newsreader's method of explaining the details.

For example, instead of 'Well, they've finally announced it. There's a meeting at the pub next week. It's about time. How long have we waited to hear about this? The local planning department are going to let us know about the proposals to re-route traffic through the town. The meeting is on Tuesday and it starts at 6 o'clock. That's not going to be a convenient time for a lot of people. I hope they've taken into consideration local people's concerns and ideas.'

Start with 'There's a meeting at the pub next Tuesday at 6pm to hear about proposals to re-route the traffic.' (The 'headline'.)

Then, and only then, elaborate, in the same way that newsreaders do:

'We've waited a long time to hear about this from the planning department. I hope they've taken local people's concerns and ideas into consideration. I'm not sure that 6 o'clock is going to be a convenient time for a lot of people.'

And, in another example, instead of this:

'I wonder, if you wouldn't mind, doing me a favour. The thing is I wouldn't normally ask, it's just that my car is out of action. I have to get into town tomorrow. Of course I would take the train but it's a rail replacement bus service. If you were free, I wonder if it would put you out? Would you mind giving me a lift ? Just say if you can't. I'll ask my neighbour if you can't do it but I know you often go into town on a Friday.'

Say this instead; 'I have favour to ask you; would you be free to give me a lift into town on Friday? (The headline.) I would take the train but it's a rail replacement bus service. If you were free that'd be great but just say if you can't and I'll ask my neighbour.'

Stating the 'headline' first introduces the subject, sets the context, and will help the other person follow you as you say more.

The Listener's Perspective

> If you talk to a man in a language he understands, that goes to his head. If you talk to him in his language, that goes to his heart.
>
> Nelson Mandela

However, even if you're clear about what you want to say, you can't assume that the other person will understand what you mean. You need to be aware that their perspective, situation, and knowledge concerning what you're talking about might be different from yours. What do they already know or not know about what you are talking about? In some situations, you might need to ask yourself 'Do they know why I'm talking about this? Do they know what or who I'm talking about?'

What might they feel about what you're talking about? Might it be a situation where they have strong feelings, values, or beliefs?

Is this a good time and place for them to listen to what you have to say? Avoid times when you're both tired, stressed, or distracted, when something else is happening or just about to happen. This doesn't mean putting off important conversations, it just means recognizing that there are times when others are more open and receptive to listening and talking about something. And if you're not sure, just ask 'when would be a good time to talk about…?'

Adapt What You Say and How You Say it

Be prepared to adapt the way you communicate when you're talking to someone. This doesn't mean that you can't be yourself, it just means being aware that what you say and how you say it can help make it easy for other people to listen and to understand what you mean.

Sophie, for example, had been seconded to another department at the company she worked for, to work with a group of colleagues on a new project. Sophie is an active communicator; she talks quite fast and she tends to interrupt if the person she's talking with is taking their time to say what they think and feel, do or don't want. In order to communicate effectively with different members of the team, Sophie knew she would have to adapt her style. She retained her friendly, enthusiastic approach, but she made a point of slowing down, which gave her time to think and explain things more clearly and concisely to her colleagues. Sophie cut small talk to a minimum when talking with colleagues who wanted to get straight to the point and discuss ideas and plans. She allowed herself more time to chat with others who enjoyed long conversations (whether they were work-related or not). She also worked out which colleagues preferred to have face-to-face meetings and which preferred to communicate via email.

Jon is a colleague of Sophie's. His communication style is very different from Sophie's. He likes to listen more than he talks. In meetings, he prefers to listen to what everyone says and then spend time afterwards reflecting on the information and ideas that the team discussed. Jon has let team members know that he needs to take notes during meetings and that he might need time to think through the issues. They've agreed it will be fine for him to follow up after the meeting with thoughts, ideas, observations, or questions by email.

How You Say it

Try and be aware of the impact that tone, pitch, emphasis, and pace can have on what you say and the extent to which the other person will understand. Do you, for example, need to slow down? Perhaps you normally speak quite quickly? Or perhaps you tend to speed up when you're nervous, excited, or stressed. Whatever the situation, slowing down will help you feel more in control and make it more likely that the other person can follow what you're saying.

Talking to someone with communication difficulties

The advice from organizations such as Action on Hearing Loss actiononhearingloss.org.uk can be followed by all of us, whether or not we are talking with a person with hearing loss. They suggest that there are four simple things you can do to make communication straightforward for both of you. (Even if someone is wearing hearing aids it doesn't mean they can hear you perfectly.)

- Speak clearly but not too slowly, and don't exaggerate your lip movements as this can make it harder to lip read.
- Use natural facial expressions and gestures.
- Don't shout. It can be uncomfortable for hearing aid users, and it looks aggressive.
- If someone doesn't understand what you've said, don't keep repeating it. Try saying it in a different way instead.

Use pauses between key phrases. It's these pauses which give listeners the chance to process what has been said. For example, saying the following sentence, word by word, with no pauses in between, is more difficult to understand than if the sentence contained a couple of pauses at key points.

- My Mum's sister is coming to visit us in London in April.

- My Mum's sister (pause) is coming to visit us (pause) in London in April.

And in another example:

- I'm going to the shops tomorrow so that I can buy a present for my friend's birthday.

If you add pauses, it makes it easier for the other person to understand what's being said.

- I'm going to the shops (pause) tomorrow (pause) so that I can buy a present (pause) for my friend's birthday.

These pauses are not so long that they disrupt the natural flow of what's being said, but just long enough to give the other person a better chance of processing what they've heard.

Pauses are especially helpful for *anyone* who may have difficulty understanding everything the talker is saying. This is especially true in noisy situations. Speaking more slowly can also be helpful for anyone whose first language is not English.

The NHS (www.nhs.uk) and the National Autistic Society (www.autism.org) also have advice for talking with people with communication difficulties.

The NHS's advice for talking with someone with dementia who has difficulty speaking or understanding, is to:

- Use short sentences to talk and ask questions.
- Keep your tone of voice positive and friendly.

- Keep a respectful distance to avoid intimidating the other person – being at the same level or lower than they are (for example, if they are sitting) can help.
- Pat or hold the person's hand while talking to them to help reassure them and make you feel closer – watch their body language and listen to what they say to see whether they're comfortable with you doing this.

The National Autistic Society says that an autistic person can find it difficult to filter out less important information; that if there is too much information, it can lead to 'overload', where no further information can be processed. They suggest that when communicating with an autistic person you may need to:

- Say less and say it slowly.
- Use specific key words, repeating and stressing them.
- Pause between words and phrases to give the person time to process what you've said, and to give them a chance to think of a response.
- Don't use too many questions.
- Be aware of the environment (noisy/crowded) that you are in. Sensory input may be affecting how much the person can process.

Remember, the advice for communicating with people with communication difficulties can be followed by all of us, whoever we're talking to. But if a person does have communication difficulties don't talk to them as if they're stupid, or as if their communication difficulties are annoying to you. It's easy to come across as condescending when speaking slowly. You just need to adapt and be patient.

Practise the Pause

If you do think you need to speak with less speed, there are ways to practise. Here's how:

- Use the beat method; count two beats at the end of every sentence. For example, 'Today is Monday.' (1,2) 'Tomorrow will be Tuesday.' (1,2)
- Read with rhythm. Practise reading song lyrics or poetry. They have a natural rhythm with built-in pauses. Pause for a comma, and use a longer pause at the end of a verse.
- Write the word 'pause' or 'breathe' on a sticky note. Place the note on your computer or near the phone, to serve as a reminder.

Top Tip

Listen to good speakers. President Obama is a master of the pause. He pauses frequently to allow others time to take in what he is saying. He slows it down, lowers his volume, and pauses for impact. At other times he speeds up his pace and raises the volume of his voice to underscore a key sentence.

Lose the Filler Words

When you're nervous, distracted, or at a loss for what to say next, you may find yourself using 'filler words' such as er, erm, um, you know, like, right. These words may give you a moment to collect your thoughts before you continue speaking; but if you overuse them, they become irritating for the listener and distract from what you're saying. And if you're hoping to come across as confident, authoritative, or persuasive, um's and ah's will have the opposite effect; they'll undermine and weaken what you're saying.

The good news is that you can turn a weakness for using filler words into a strength by replacing fillers with pauses. Of course, even the briefest pause can feel like an interminable silence, but well-placed pauses can make you sound calm and collected. If, when you're speaking, you lose your train of thought, a pause gives you time to get back on track. As long as the pause isn't too long (no more than five seconds) it won't come across as strange or unnatural.

Top Tip

If you'd like to replace filler words with pauses, try the following. Describe out loud what you did from the beginning to the end of yesterday. Practise using pauses instead of filler words as you recall the events.

Avoid Using Jargon

As well as being aware of and using fewer filler words, do avoid using jargon. Jargon uses words and phrases which are unique to a small group of people – usually in a particular job or profession – as a kind of shorthand.

Such jargon is fine if you know that the person you're talking to understands it, but it's inconsiderate, unhelpful, and confusing for them if they don't.

For example, a reference to 'Meds' (Medication) or 'Obs' (Obstetrics) will make sense to a healthcare professional but if the person listening doesn't come from a health background the other person needs to explain the reference. And the acronym – 'CPN' could mean one of two things. To a healthcare worker it would mean Community Psychiatric Nurse. But for a police officer, it would mean Community Protection Notice. And the rest of us would probably have no idea what either of them were talking about!

Jargon is OK when it represents a concise way of saying something to people who can make sense of it, but not when it's a substitute for easily understood words. Always put yourself in the place of the listener and if you think they may not understand, explain the jargon in ordinary words. So a healthcare worker might say, for example, to a patient, 'You might find it helpful to make an appointment with the CPN (the jargon) – the Community Psychiatric Nurse – (the explanation) to talk about how you're feeling.'

Wise men speak because they have something to say, fools because they have to say something.

Plato

Avoid using gobbledygook terms such as 'comfort break' rather than 'break', 'blue sky thinking' for 'clear thinking', 'citizen empowerment' for 'people power', 'slippage' rather than 'delay'. It's not big and it's not clever. It's contrived and confusing. Talk proper English!

Letter to *The Times*, March 2019

I note the Duke of Sussex's new communications chief once 'oversaw global corporate accounts with a particular emphasis on executive thought leadership and purpose led campaigns'.

Google translate struggled to inform me what this meant. Can anyone help? I am sure the Duke would also like to know before he signs the contract.

Ian Tinsley, Warminster, Wiltshire

Invite Questions and Feedback

No matter how clear and concise you might be, sometimes you can't be sure if the other person has understood, not necessarily because they've told you, but from their facial expression. Perhaps their expression doesn't appropriately reflect or match what you're saying; you're telling them something amusing, for example, but they're looking angry or upset, confused or concerned.

Instead of rattling on, simply ask 'What do you think?' or 'How does that sound?' Or 'I'm not sure if I'm being clear, can you tell me what you understood?'

Asking questions is also useful when you think the other person isn't listening. Simply ask them a direct question. Simply say, 'What do you think'? or 'Would you agree?' Then when they look at you blankly, just repeat the question and add the topic you were talking about: '*What do you think* we should do for Mum's birthday'? or '*Do you agree* that the Elgin Marbles should be returned to Greece?'

Make it easy for other people to listen and to understand what you mean. Communicate purposefully; take time to think before you speak. Be more aware of what you say, how you say it, and when you say it.

In a nutshell

- There's one rule: say what you mean. Be clear and direct, in a way that makes it easy for other people to listen and to understand what you mean.
- Hit the headline first. Think about what the main point is that you need to make. You should be able to say it in one or two sentences. Then elaborate and explain the details.

- Even if you're clear about what you want to say, their perspective or knowledge concerning what you're talking about might be different from yours. What do they already know or not know about what you're talking about? What might they feel about what you're talking about? Is this a good time and place for them to listen to what you have to say?
- Be prepared to adapt the way you communicate when you're talking to someone; be aware that how you say it can help make it easy for other people to listen and to understand what you mean.
- Do you, for example, need to slow down? Slowing down will help make it more likely that the other person can follow what you're saying. So, pause at meaningful places so that their ears can catch up with your mouth.
- The advice for communicating with someone with communication difficulties can be followed by all of us, whoever we're talking to. But if a person does have communication difficulties don't talk to them as if they're stupid, or as if their communication difficulties are annoying to you. You just need to adapt and be patient.
- If you overuse filler words such as 'um' and 'er' they become irritating for the listener and distract from what you're saying. Try replacing fillers with pauses. In contrast to filler words, pauses can help you feel and sound calm, confident, and collected.

- Avoid using jargon and gobbledygook terms. Jargon is inconsiderate, unhelpful, and confusing for someone if they don't understand it. Gobbledygook is contrived and confusing. Talk proper English!
- No matter how clear and concise you might be, sometimes you can't be sure if the other person has understood. Instead of rattling on, simply ask 'What do you think?' or 'How does that sound?'

3
Putting it in Writing

Just as you do when you're talking to someone, when you put something in writing you need to make it easy for the other person – the reader – to understand you. When you're talking with another person – in person or on the phone – you can get an immediate response from that person, and if there are any obvious misunderstandings you're able to clarify what you mean. But when you communicate in writing this doesn't necessarily happen, so you need to be even more sure to make your meaning clear.

To communicate effectively, to write what you mean, and to make sure the other person understands you, follow the following guidelines:

Hit the headline. Just as when you're communicating in speech, think about what the main point is that you need to make. Put it in a sentence. Then provide details that spell out what, where, who, when, and why.

Get straight to the point, keep to the point, and avoid making the reader work for the point. Most of us receive too many communications: letters, emails, adverts, junk mail. Letters, emails, reports, etc that ramble or are vague will not be read properly. In contrast, written communications that are concise can be understood quickly. So be short. Once you've decided what your main point is, decide what the reader does, and, just as importantly, doesn't need to know.

Write it more than once. The advantage of communicating in writing is that you can edit your message so that it conveys exactly what you want to say. So, write a first draft to include everything that you want to say. At this stage, don't aim for perfection as you go. You'll get stuck. Instead, just get your ideas out of your head and down on paper or the screen. Once you've got it all down, then rewrite it to ensure that your message is clear. It's much easier to edit something you've already written than to edit as you write. Trying to get it word perfect the first time will block the ideas you have about what you want to say. So, write a first draft, *then* work on getting your points in the right order, with the right words, spelling, and grammar.

Avoid repeating anything, other than for emphasis. Decide what to remove. There'll always be something.

Clarity comes with simple words and short sentences. Cut out unnecessary words and phrases. Instead of, for example, 'I'm quite confident and definitely believe that the event will be a very successful one' write

'I'm confident the event will succeed'. The second sentence is both shorter and stronger.

And instead of, 'I would be extremely grateful if you could take the time to send me…' write 'Please could you send me…'. And, instead of 'in the normal course of events' use 'normally'.

So, remove unnecessary words from every sentence, unnecessary sentences from every paragraph, and unnecessary paragraphs entirely. There's no shame in not getting it right the first time; even professional writers follow this process – they write down their ideas and then they rewrite until they are happy that what they have written is clear and concise, in a logical order and conveys what they want to say.

Do keep related information together. Don't move on to another point until you've finished the last, and resist the urge to move back and forth between topics or issues. Otherwise you'll come across as rambling with no sense of focus.

Don't take being concise too far. Just as when you're talking face to face or on the phone, you can't assume that the other person will understand what you mean. You need to be aware that their perspective, situation, and knowledge concerning what you're talking about might be different from yours. What do they already know or not know about what you are talking about? In some situations, you might need to ask yourself, 'Do they know *why* I'm talking about this? Do they know what or who I'm talking about?'

Top Tip

Give examples. If you put forward an idea, try and follow it up with an example, to help the reader understand what you mean: 'I think we could do with some fresh perspectives' could be followed with 'we could, for example, invite the interns to the meetings and ask for their ideas'.

Mind your language. Whoever you're writing to it's important to use language – words and phrases – that is inclusive; that anyone can understand. The advice for communicating with people in speech is the same as for communicating in writing. Avoid jargon and gobbledygook.

Defending Against Drivel

The Plain English Campaign (www.plainenglish.co.uk) has helped many government departments and other official organizations with their documents, reports, and publications, helping them make sure their public information is as clear as possible. They define plain English as 'writing that the intended audience can read, understand and act upon the first time they read it'. They also describe plain English as

---

'a message, written with the reader in mind and with the right tone of voice, that is clear and concise'.

They have recently announced the availability of Drivel Defence, a software package that will help you to check the use of plain English. It includes the following two tools; Drivel Defence for Text and Drivel Defence for Web.

Drivel Defence for Text allows you to check text by copying it from any software or document. It's ideal for letters or reports. You can use Drivel Defence for Text from the Plain English website, or you can download it and run it on your own computer.

Drivel Defence for Web is a tool specifically to help website developers check whether the content of web pages is in plain English. To use it you must download it and run it on your own computer.

Both programs can give you a detailed report on your use of Plain English, but neither makes any changes. This leaves you in control. Use them to keep drivel at bay.

Top Tip

Collect examples of good writing – what do you like and dislike? Don't just look at the content – the words and phrases that are used. Look at the layout too. What makes something easy to read?

Rambling, hinting, implying, and alluding are indirect ways to say something; they hide the meaning of what you really want to say. The best way to make it easy for others to read and understand is to be clear, direct, and concise. So, before you send it, ask yourself if your message was clear; did you say what you wanted to say? Don't make the reader have to work to understand your letter or email; make it easy to understand and to reply to.

In a nutshell

- Just as you do when you're talking to someone, when you put something in writing you need to make it easy for the other person – the reader – to understand you.
- Once you've decided what your main point is, decide what the reader does, and, just as importantly, doesn't need to know.
- Be aware that the reader's perspective, situation, and knowledge concerning what you're talking about might be different from yours. What background information might you need to give?
- It's much easier to edit something you've already written than to edit as you write. Trying to get it word perfect the first time will block the ideas you have about what you want to say.

- So, write a first draft, *then* work on getting your points in the right order, with the right words, removing unnecessary words, correcting spelling and grammar. Just like professional writers do; they write down their ideas and then they rewrite until they are happy that what they have written is clear and concise, in a logical order, and conveys what they want to say.

4
Being a Better Listener

I like to listen. I have learned a great deal from listening carefully.

Ernest Hemingway

How well do you listen? Do you usually find it easy to pay attention and understand what someone else is saying? Or are there often times when you *think* you've listened and understood only to find out that actually, you hadn't. You'd misunderstood; because of your own biases and assumptions, prejudices and judgements you'd distorted the meaning of what the other person was saying.

Perhaps there are times when you know you've listened – you've been paying attention – but you don't understand what the other person is talking about; you're trying to make sense of what they're saying but it's not clear and you're confused.

And of course there are times when you know you're *not* listening and taking in what the other person has said because you're thinking about something else – maybe you're thinking about what you want to say – or you're distracted by something, or the other person is boring, or they're repeating themselves, or they're being critical or offensive in some way.

Active, Reflective Listening

There are so many situations – at work, in social situations, for example – where being a better listener can help you to better connect to others. The way to become an effective listener is to learn and practise active listening. It's called 'active' listening because you're active in the process of listening; you don't just hear what's being said, you *do* something; you put some effort into acknowledging and understanding the other person's perspective and what they mean.

Active listening starts with reflective listening. Reflective listening involves repeating, paraphrasing, and summarizing.

Repeating. When you're repeating, you're simply saying *exactly* what the other person has just said. For example, 'Yes, it *is* nice here. I agree, it would be a shame to have to leave', or 'You *weren't* calling me stupid?'

All you're doing is repeating what you've heard to make sure, or to show that you heard it correctly. This is the same as when someone gives you directions on how to get to another part of town or tells you a phone number – you are simply repeating the directions or the numbers back to the other person so that they can confirm you've understood correctly.

And, just like when you repeat directions or a phone number, you're not necessarily agreeing with what the other person has said. You're just confirming that you have listened and understood.

Summarizing. This involves briefly and concisely summing up what the other person has said; the main points. For example 'So, you're saying that you're not sure if you can join us that weekend. And even if you can, you think the hotel we're going to book won't be suitable for your needs. Is that right?'

Paraphrasing. This is a restatement of what the other person has said as you understood it. For example 'I think what you're saying is that I expect too much and that some members of the team are feeling that nothing they do is ever good enough. Is that right?'

When you paraphrase, it's a good idea to begin with a phrase such as:

- 'Let me see if I understand so far...'
- 'Am I right in thinking that you've said/you feel/you mean...?'
- 'I think what you're saying is...'
- 'Are you saying... or are you saying...?'

With both paraphrasing and summarizing, you express, in your own words, your understanding of what the other person said and you end by asking 'Is that what you said?' or 'Is that right?'

Reflecting in this way gives the other person the opportunity to confirm that this *is* what they've said. It also allows them to refute or clarify what they've said. For example, you might say, 'It sounds like you're disappointed.' They might then agree, that yes, they are disappointed, or that no, they're not disappointed, they're actually very upset!

Top Tip

It's worth noting that there are times when overstating or understating a reflection can be effective in getting a person to clarify or reconsider. For example, if someone felt you didn't listen properly, in order to get them to clarify, you might overstate what they said by saying 'You think I *always* interrupt and I *never* listen. Is that what you said?' And if you think someone is anxious about a forthcoming event, you might say 'So you're feeling a little unsure. Or is it more than that?'

In a range of situations when you're listening to someone else, first and foremost, your aim should be to understand what the other person is saying. The two examples below illustrate how the listener is actively listening – repeating, summarizing, and paraphrasing.

First example:

> **Ella:** I don't know what to do; I've been offered two jobs! It's a problem that I'm lucky to have, but it's still a problem. They're both good jobs and both of them have their pros and cons. I've gone over and over it but I still can't decide which job I should take. I need to make my decision by Friday.
>
> **Josh:** You've been offered *two* good jobs? (Repeating)
>
> **Ella:** Yep!
>
> **Josh:** And you've only got two more days left to decide? (Paraphrasing)
>
> **Ella:** Yes! The first job is better paid but it's longer hours. The second job is less well paid but there's better opportunities for promotion. But the first job is in a good environment and easier to get to from where I live. Oh, yes, I forgot to say, the second job could involve trips to the head office in New York every now and then. I've never been to New York. My friend Jay says I should go for the first job. But I'm not sure.
>
> **Josh:** So, the first job is better paid, it's in a good environment, and easier to get to from where you live. But it's longer hours. The second job is less pay but there's better opportunities for promotion and could involve trips to New York. (Summarizing)
>
> **Ella:** Exactly.

Second example:

> **Ali:** Our next-door neighbour got a puppy last year. Everything was OK for the first few months but then it seems that the novelty of having a dog wore off.

I don't think they take it for a walk very often any more. In fact I'm not sure that they ever take it out!

Rose: They *never* take it out? (Repeating)

Ali: Well, hardly ever. And the thing is, the dog is sent out the back to do its business, it barks from the minute it gets outside until it's brought back in, usually with the door being slammed. It's a small dog and has a sharp, yappy bark which wakes us up early in the morning.

I've recently started working from home. Throughout the day the poor thing is barking in the house when it is left on its own. It can be on its own from 8.30 am until 3.30 in the afternoon. I feel bad for the dog but I don't know how to approach the subject with my neighbour. We are on OK terms and I don't want to cause a rift or ill-feeling between us.

Rose: So let me get this right – the dog's barking and the door being slammed wakes you up early in the morning. It then gets left in the house and you can hear it barking all day. (Summarizing) Does the barking bother you or is it more that you're worried about the dog?

Ali: The barking is getting on my nerves *and* I'm worried about him.

In both these examples you can see how active listening from the other person helps the speaker feel understood and encourages further conversation. Of course, it would be quite odd to repeat, summarize, or paraphrase what someone said every time they spoke to you! The point is – and this is a crucial point – to listen *as if* you were going to reflect back. Whether you do so or not. This is why *reflective listening* is so powerful. It focuses your attention, stops you from interrupting, helps you to listen and be clear about what the other person is actually saying.

Top Tip

Tell yourself that you'll tell someone else about this conversation later on. A good way to make sure you stay tuned in and listen is to imagine that you are going to repeat what you learned to someone else. Then you'll be more alert and more likely to ask questions to ensure that you understand what the other person is saying.

Listen for Feelings

As the other person is describing their experience, explaining their point of view, making their case etc, listen for feelings and how their feelings link to the situation or experience that they're talking about.

Imagine, for example, that Asha is telling you about a business deal he's successfully pulled off and how impressed his colleagues were. At one point you say, 'You're obviously happy because you've earned a good bonus from the deal, but it sounds like you're even more pleased that you proved to your colleagues that you're capable of handling a deal that size on your own!' And Asha replies, 'Yes. That's exactly right! I knew I could do it, but others weren't so sure.'

And, in another example, when Ben is ranting to you about an episode with his manager, you might respond with:

'So you're still fuming. Your manager blaming you for something you didn't do was bad enough. But doing it in front of the customer left you feeling humiliated. Is that right?'

Practise Active Listening

Becoming a good listener takes time, patience, and concentration. It also takes practice. You can practise with a friend. Here's how:

One of you talks for two minutes on one of the subjects below. When the speaker has finished speaking, the listener can reflect back what he or she thinks the speaker said and how they felt:

- The best job or holiday you ever had
- The worst job or holiday you ever had
- A pet you once had
- Your thoughts about the Royal Family
- What you'd do if you won ten million pounds
- A time when you were disappointed – you didn't get the place on the course, the job, house, flat, you wanted.

Top Tip

Active listening is a skill that you can easily improve; the more you practise, the better you get at it. Listen to someone explain something in a podcast. Practise summarizing and paraphrasing what they said.

Top Tip

What happens if you can't listen? If you are too busy, distracted, confused, or worried to focus on what the speaker is saying? Say so! Explain that this isn't a good time for you. Tell the other person or agree a time when you will be more able to give your full attention.

Communicating with someone with memory loss

The NHS website – www.nhs.co.uk – has advice for listening to someone with dementia:

- Stop what you're doing so you can give the person your full attention while they speak.
- Minimize distractions that may get in the way of communication, such as the television or the radio playing too loudly, but always check if it's OK to do so.

- You may need to be more aware of non-verbal messages, such as facial expressions and body language.
- You may have to use more physical contact, such as reassuring pats on the arm, or smile as well as speaking.
- Use eye contact to look at the person, and encourage them to look at you when either of you are talking.
- Try not to interrupt them, even if you think you know what they're saying.
- Repeat what you heard back to the person and ask if it's accurate, or ask them to repeat what they said.

The Alzheimers Society – www.alzheimers.org.uk – adds the following advice:

- If you haven't understood fully, rephrase what you have understood and check to see if you are right. The person's reaction and body language can be a good indicator of what they've understood and how they feel.
- If the person with dementia has difficulty finding the right word or finishing a sentence, ask them to explain it in a different way. Listen out for clues. Also pay attention to their body language. The expression on their face and the way they hold themselves can give you clear signals about how they are feeling.
- Allow the person plenty of time to respond – it may take them longer to process the information

and work out their response. Don't interrupt the person as it can break the pattern of communication.

- If a person is feeling sad, let them express their feelings. Do not dismiss a person's worries – sometimes the best thing to do is just listen, and show that you are there.

Ask Questions

> Seek first to understand, then to be understood.
> Stephen Covey

As well as helping you to pay attention to what someone is saying, active listening is helpful when you don't understand; you're more likely to ask questions to get a better understanding, to clarify and verify what was said. Asking questions also shows that you're interested in knowing more about what's being said.

Asking questions also helps you to avoid or overcome assumptions and open yourself up to other possibilities. When you make assumptions and judgements, you close off avenues of understanding. But when you're curious, you are more open to learning and developing a connection. If, for example, a friend told you 'I slept with my ex' your assumptions about either person, their past relationship, intentions, behaviour, and so on might make you react with 'I can't believe it. I didn't think you'd ever see her again!' But saying this just results in the other person defending their actions and hinders communication between you.

Instead you might ask, 'How did that happen?' which withholds any judgement and opens up the lines of communication. You can minimize your assumptions and judgement by making curiosity your default setting. Give others the benefit of the doubt; ask questions to learn more.

Open and Closed Questions

There are two types of questions: open questions and closed questions. Open questions usually begin with the words what, why, how, tell me, explain, and describe. For example; 'Tell me more about...' 'How did...?' 'Why do you think...?' 'And how did you feel about that?' 'What's the problem with...?' 'Can you tell me...? 'What did you think about that?'

When you ask open questions you encourage the other person to explain more. On the other hand, closed questions, such as 'Are you upset?' and 'Don't you want to do it?' usually get a short response: 'Yes' or 'No'. Open questions invite a person to express in their own words their ideas, thoughts, opinions, and feelings.

Look at how the examples below compare open and closed questions. In each example, the issue is the same, but the responses will be different:

1. Do you want to do this next?
   What do you want to do next?
2. Would you like things to be different?
   How would you like things to be different?
3. Shall I help you with...?
   How can I help you with...?
4. Is it a problem?
   In what ways might this be a problem?
5. Are you feeling better today?
   How are you feeling?
6. Can I help you with that?
   How can I help you?
7. Can you make it happen?
   How do you see this happening?

When you ask open questions, do make sure you give the other person enough time to answer. They may need to think before they say something so don't see a pause as an opportunity for you to jump in with your ideas and opinions! Let the other person finish each point before you ask questions. Interrupting is a waste of time. It can distract and frustrate them. But once they have replied, you might need to summarize or paraphrase their answer before you continue with your response.

Top Tip

Don't be afraid to ask questions. Asking questions does not make you look stupid. Being too shy to ask what something means doesn't help anyone. Listen

---

to news programmes and chat shows on the radio and TV. Note how often the interviewer confidently asks questions to clarify both their own and the listener's understanding.

Top Tip

Do ask questions in terms of feelings. Don't just ask 'What do/did you think?' or 'What are you going to do?' When it's relevant, ask 'How do/did you *feel* about that?' Asking questions in term of feelings can give you a better insight into their behaviour, their motivations and intentions. And be aware of your non-verbal communication when you're asking questions. Be sure that your questions don't come across as interrogative, attacking, defensive, rude. Your body language and tone of voice all play a part in the response you get when you ask questions.

Funnel Questions

Open questions can be asked using a method known as 'funnel questioning'. Funnel questions are a series of questions that seek further information that either goes into more detail or become more general.

Funnel questions that increase detail give you, the listener, more information about fewer topics. You start with general questions, and then narrow in on a point in each answer, gathering more detail with each question. For example:

Kris: Can you *tell me* about the meeting?
Paul: I think it went quite well. There were just a couple of problems.
Kris: What, *specifically*, was one of the problems?
Paul: We couldn't agree a date for completion.
Kris: What date, *exactly*, did she suggest?
Paul: The 15th of next month.

Asking 'tell me about...' is a general, open question. According to the other person's response, you the listener, can then pick up on and ask further questions to find out increasing detail about some particular topic of interest. This narrows the funnel, giving you more information about a smaller area.

Using focus words like 'specifically', 'exactly', or 'particularly' directs the speaker to explain a particular point, in more detail. Use these along with 'what', 'how' and 'when'.

For example: 'You said that she wasn't happy about leaving it to the end of the month. What, specifically, did she say?'

Top Tip

Listen to the BBC Radio 4 programme 'The Choice' to hear how funnel questions work in gathering information that narrows down the details.

Funnel questions that increase detail give you, the listener, more information about fewer topics. In contrast, funnel questions that decrease asking for details broaden out the questions to give you wider information about more general topics. Asking questions that begin, for example, with 'Who else' and 'What else'. For example: 'So, she accepted the end of the month as a completion date. *What else* did you discuss?'

This style of questioning can be useful in situations where you want to encourage the person you're speaking with to open up.

Closed Questions

Open questions encourage the other person to explain more; to express in their own words their ideas, thoughts, opinions, and feelings. In contrast, closed questions usually get a short response. Often, when you ask a closed question, it's likely that you will need to ask another question. And if you use too many close-ended questions, it can be difficult to carry on a proper conversation.

For example, the following exchange is less of a conversation and more of an interrogation:

Did you want to go?
Not really.
Can you afford to go?
No.
Do you know what you'll do next?
Nope.

Do your friends know?
Probably.
Do you think they'll help you?
I'm not sure.

There are, though, times when a series of closed questions like those in the example above, are appropriate. Closed questions are quick and easy to answer and helpful when you just need to obtain facts and get a straightforward answer: 'Are you cold?' 'Does it hurt?' 'Are you upset?' 'Don't you want to do it?'

And as the last four examples illustrate, closed questions are easier and less stressful for someone to answer when they're upset, angry, confused, or stressed in some way.

Closed questions are also good for checking your understanding, or the other person's: 'So, if I get this qualification, I will get a raise?' and in another example: 'You're saying she won't do it? Is that right?' And closed questions can help when concluding a discussion or making a decision: 'Now we know the facts, are we all agreed this is the right course of action?'

Closed questions can be less challenging to answer for someone with a communication difficulty. The National Autistic Society says that some people on the autistic spectrum may struggle with open-ended questions. Therefore, they suggest you ask specific, closed questions. For example, ask 'Did you have a good day?' or 'Do you like maths?' rather than 'How was your day?' or 'Can you tell me which subjects you like to study?' They advise that you ask only the most necessary questions and keep questions short and that you structure your questions to offer options or choices. For example, 'Would you like to go today or tomorrow?'

So, although, in a range of situations, closed questions can be quick and easy to answer, in other circumstances and situations, a closed question can inhibit conversation and lead to an awkward silence, or lead conversation to a dead end.

Rhetorical Questions

Closed questions can also be used for deceptive purposes; to lead the other person to your way of thinking. One way of doing this is by framing ideas and opinions as rhetorical questions. Rhetorical questions aren't really questions at all, in that they don't require an answer. They are a persuasive technique, used to lead the other person to your way of thinking.

Rhetorical questions are statements phrased in question form:

'If you don't revise for the exam, how will you ever succeed?'
'Do you agree that we need to do something about global warming?'

Rhetorical questions can be effective in engaging the listener; they are more likely to agree than if they were simply told something: 'You need to revise' and 'We need to do something about global warming.' Any opinion can be turned into a closed question that forces a yes or no answer (and gets agreement) by adding tag questions at the end of the sentence such as 'isn't it?', 'don't you?', or 'won't they'? For example, 'The cheaper option is better, isn't it?' and 'You all agree, don't you?'

Rhetorical questions can also be framed in such a way that they are both quick and easy to answer, giving you the answer you want, while leaving the other person assuming they've had a choice. For example, 'Do you want to eat the broccoli before you eat your sausages or after you eat your sausages?' (Useful for getting young children to comply!)

If you use them in a self-serving way or one that undermines the interests of the other person, you're being manipulative and dishonest. On the other hand, closed, leading questions can be used positively; when managing, mentoring, or coaching for example. Closed questions can help get someone else to consider and agree with your suggestions. For example, 'Wouldn't it be great to get some qualifications?'

The Rhetorical Question Mark

A printer from the sixteenth century, Henry Denham, invented the rhetorical question mark, '⸮', which was a question mark facing the opposite direction. However, it never became a permanent punctuation mark in the English language.

Top Tip

Identify and learn from good listeners. Can you think of someone you know who's a good listener? Why do think they're good listeners? How do they show they've listened and understood what someone else has said? What questions do they ask?

The Benefits of Active Listening

There are so many ways that active listening makes communication easier and helps you better connect with others. Active listening enables you to:

Concentrate on what the other person is saying. Whether or not you reflect back to the other person what they said, because you are listening *as if* you were going to reflect back, active listening compels you to concentrate. Furthermore, active listening prevents you from being distracted by whatever else may be going on in or around you. It helps you avoid thinking about what you are going to say next (particularly helpful in conflict situations or disagreements).

Adapt your communication style. If you're an active communicator, you prefer to talk and do things more than listen and sit still. Active listening gives you something to do! For purposeful communicators, active listening gives you a purpose; the purpose being to be sure you're clear and understand what the other person means. If your preferred way of communicating is that of a theorist, active listening encourages you to clarify other people's ideas, understand their points of view, and take feelings into account. And if you're more of a connecter? Well, you're probably already a good listener!

Increase your understanding. Active listening helps you to interpret what the other person has said, in your own words. Reflecting back and asking relevant questions allows the speaker to confirm that you have or haven't understood.

Be more likely to remember what was said later. Active listening is mindful listening. With active listening, you're more present – you're focused and engaged.

Avoid being bored. Active listening helps you to engage with what the speaker is saying; to look for points of interest.

Be deterred from interrupting. You don't interrupt and break into what the other person is saying with unnecessary questions or comments. You recognize that interrupting is a waste of time; it frustrates the speaker and can limit your understanding of what they want to say.

Overcome your assumptions. Your assumptions, emotions, judgements, and beliefs can distort what the other person has said. With active listening, the other person can confirm or refute your interpretation and help you see things from their point of view. They are less likely to feel judged and will feel OK about explaining what they think and why.

Encourage the speaker to open up. When you show that you really are listening, you encourage the other person to open up and say more.

Develop empathy and rapport. Active listening and empathy are mutually inclusive. By trying to understand what the other person is saying and feeling, you are trying to see things from their point of view.

Improve your ability to influence, persuade, and negotiate. Active listening increases your understanding of the person's intentions, feelings, and motivations. So, you're more likely to respond appropriately and say whatever is necessary to strengthen negotiation, diplomacy, and cooperation.

Identify areas of agreement as well as disagreement. When areas of agreement are recognized, they can put disagreements into perspective and diminish their significance, making for more positive and effective communication. The speaker is also more likely to identify flaws in their reasoning when they hear it objectively summarized by the listener.

Consider different points of view. When a person knows their opinion is being heard and acknowledged, it is likely that they'll be more willing to consider an alternative point of view. Listening attentively helps each person to gain a clear understanding of the other person's point of view and move forward toward a successful solution.

Defuse conflict. When a person is being properly listened to, there's less chance of conflict escalating. Active listening allows the person to freely vent their feelings and concerns without interruption or contradiction.

Feel more in control in difficult situations. Reflecting back slows everything down. This gives both sides time to think.

In a nutshell

- When a person isn't listened to, they're likely to not have been understood. And when misunderstood, the connection between them and the other person is broken.
- The way to become an effective listener is to learn and practise active listening. Active listening is like calculating or recalling something; you need to put in some effort.
- It would be quite odd to repeat, summarize, or paraphrase what someone said every time they spoke to you! The point is – and this is a crucial point – to listen as if you were going to reflect back. Whether you do so or not.
- This is why reflective listening is so powerful. It focuses your attention, stops you from interrupting, helps you to listen and be clear about what the other person is actually saying.
- With active listening you're more likely to ask questions to get a better understanding to clarify and verify what was said.
- Asking questions helps you to avoid or overcome assumptions and open yourself up to other

---

possibilities; to show that you're interested in knowing more about what's being said.

- When you ask open questions you encourage the other person to explain more. Closed questions usually get a short response – 'Yes' or 'No' – and can lead conversation down a dead end. However, in a range of situations, closed questions are appropriate because they are quick and easy to answer.

- Rhetorical questions aren't really questions at all, in that they don't require an answer. They are a persuasive technique, used to lead the other person to your way of thinking.

- There are many ways that active listening makes communication easier and helps you better connect with others. Amongst other things, active listening enables you to: concentrate on what the other person is saying and avoid interrupting; overcome your assumptions and increase your understanding; develop empathy and rapport; consider different points of view; and be clear about where you do and don't agree.

5
Reading Between
the Lines

So when you are listening to somebody, completely, attentively, then you are listening not only to the words, but also to the feeling of what is being conveyed, to the whole of it, not part of it.

Jiddu Krishnamurti

Becoming a better listener will help you better connect with others; you'll improve your understanding of other people's perspectives: what they think, how they feel, and what they mean. But it's not just what a person says that tells you what they're thinking and feeling. What a person doesn't say – their non-verbal communication – can often give you a clearer insight into what's going on; it can emphasize and support what someone is saying. It can also contradict what they're saying.

You may have come across the claim that communication is made up of 7% what is said, 38% how it's said, and 55% body language. But this is not entirely accurate. Professor Albert Mehrabian, whose work on communication is the source of these statistics, has stated that this is a misunderstanding of the findings. 'My percentage numbers apply only when a person is communicating about *emotions* and definitely do not apply to communication in general.'

For example, with the spoken instruction 'Go to the end of the street and turn left', there's no hidden message. The words carry 100% of the meaning. In contrast, imagine someone asks, 'Are you still angry with me?' and the other person snaps back 'No. I'm not', with tightly folded arms and avoiding eye contact. Would you believe that they're not angry? It's unlikely. And that's because how the person *really* feels has been conveyed by their non-verbal communication.

Mehrabian's research confirmed that when words and non-verbal messages are in conflict, people believe the non-verbal every time. So, when someone is telling you what they *feel* about something, a big part of what they're communicating comes from an unconscious display of their 'silent' language; which either reinforces, detracts, or contradicts what they are saying.

Speech is mostly conscious and intentional. In contrast, non-verbal communication is mostly unconscious and unintentional. Mostly, you're unaware how much you're conveying non-verbally, but non-verbal communication often reveals your thoughts, feelings, and emotions more genuinely than what you say. And when you're listening to other people, you're reading or picking up on their non-verbal communication without being aware of it.

Often, you know what someone is feeling just by looking at their face; you don't need them to explain in words if they're experiencing one of the basic emotions – surprise, anger, joy, disgust, fear, or sadness. But it's not just facial expressions that can clue you in to how someone else is feeling. Other non-verbal communication – the gestures that people use, their posture, the way they sit or stand, and the extent to which they do or don't come into physical contact with others – can tell you a lot about their feelings, intentions, and motivations. Physical reactions such as fast breathing, blushing, or turning pale also communicate something to other people. So do changes in how we speak: our tone of voice, loudness, speed of talking, pauses, and silences.

> Interestingly, when communication is difficult our body language becomes more pronounced. It doesn't take you long to be sure that someone is angry if they are using short, sharp gestures.

Making Sense and Meaning of Non-Verbal Communication

However, it's not always clear what someone's gestures or facial expressions mean. A frown, for instance, can be a sign of concentration or it could indicate confusion or disapproval. So, just how can you make sense of a person's body language, gestures, facial expressions, tone of voice etc? The important thing to know is that you can't rely on a *single* gesture, facial expression, and so on to confirm what someone does or doesn't mean or what they're feeling. The key to understanding non-verbal communication is to be aware of and interpret the *combination* – the clusters – of non-verbal actions.

Clusters are when a number of non-verbal communications and actions occur close together and so indicate a consistent message. Clusters and combinations of non-verbal communications provide a much more reliable indication of what's going on. A single body language signal isn't as reliable as several signals, so do look out for a number of signs that all seem to add up to 'saying' one thing.

For example, imagine you observed someone for a few seconds and you saw their arms were tightly crossed and they were sharply nodding and shaking their head in response to what the other person was telling them. You might conclude that they were irritated or annoyed. Keep watching and you might then see them stamping their feet, and when they uncrossed their arms, they were blowing into their cupped hands. You would probably then conclude that actually, they were feeling very cold!

Be aware whether what someone says matches or is at odds with their non-verbal behaviour. Imagine, for instance, that you asked a friend if they'd like to go out to eat and they replied 'Yeah. OK.' You're not sure though that they really do want to eat out so you ask, 'Are you sure?' Your friend replies, 'I said "OK" didn't I?' But the fact that you noticed a frown on their face before they said 'Yeah. OK.' leaves you unconvinced.

Why are you unconvinced? Because you've picked up on the mismatch between verbal and non-verbal messages; you're sensing their reluctance because their verbal communication – what they say – doesn't match their non-verbal communication.

This mismatch is known as 'leakage'. Leakage occurs when a person says one thing but their body language, gestures, and so on leak something different. It's unconscious; they won't be aware of it, but if *you* fail to recognize these clues, you risk being misled, misunderstanding what someone is really thinking and feeling. So, when you think that someone isn't coming across as honest or 'real' it's probably because their non-verbal communication doesn't match what they're saying. This mismatch creates a sense of confusion and distrust.

Understanding body language can be seen as a form of mind reading! If you can read the body language, you are reading – or getting an insight into – the real feelings and thoughts. With any one of us, whatever's happening on the inside can be reflected on the outside. Even when we're silent.

Intuition

Picking up on a combination of non-verbal signs in a particular situation can also be seen as your intuition. Intuition is an unconscious process of tuning in and responding to a combination of non-verbal information in a specific context.

For example, imagine a parent asking her teenage son: 'You *will* be home by midnight won't you?' If her son turns away from her and vehemently replies: 'Yeah yeah. You've asked me twice. *Stop* going on about it', the parent might not believe her son. Why? Because when someone is being dishonest, their non-verbal behaviour is likely to change from what is normal for them; their 'baseline' behaviour. In this example, the son's way of speaking is normally calm and he makes eye contact. This time he raises his voice and looks away. The parent intuitively doesn't trust her son!

Furthermore, when people aren't being honest, they may rehearse the words they use, but not their body language. So when their body language says something different from their words, you know you're not getting the whole truth.

Look for the bigger picture as well as the details. Then, if you're in the situation where you don't believe what someone is saying, when it doesn't ring true or feel right, you will know it's because that particular combination of verbal, non-verbal, and contextual cues doesn't add up.

Learn to 'Read' Other People

You can practise 'reading' other people. Turn off the sound on your TV. Watch people being interviewed on the news. Observe people interacting in dramas and soap operas. Be aware of the non-verbal communication; the gestures, facial expressions, tone of voice, and so on.

What conclusions do you draw from particular *combinations* of non-verbal communication?

Look for combinations that support your assumptions. If you decide that, for example, someone looks defensive – ask yourself why you think that. Is it because they have a glaring stare? Because their shoulders are hunched up?

People-watching is also good not just for understanding individual people's attitudes and feelings, but also for developing your understanding of group dynamics. As well as watching people on TV, use the time that you have to wait in queues at the bus stop, supermarket, and so on to watch how people communicate and interact with each other. Observe people on the bus or the train or in a café or a bar and notice how they act and react to each other. Try to guess what they are saying and get a sense of what's going on between them.

Don't though get too caught up analysing the other person's body language; and don't always assume you've correctly interpreted their non-verbal communication; remember to listen and ask questions!

Using non-verbal communication with someone with dementia

The Alzheimers Society www.alzheimers.org.uk advises that non-verbal communication is very important for someone with dementia, and as their condition progresses it will become one of the main ways the person communicates. You can learn to recognize what a person is communicating through their body language, supporting them to remain engaged and contributing to their quality of life.

- A person with dementia will be able to read your body language. Sudden movements or a tense facial expression may cause upset or distress, and can make communication more difficult.
- Make sure that your body language and facial expression match what you are saying.
- Never stand too close to someone or stand over them to communicate – it can feel intimidating. Instead, respect the person's personal space and drop to or below their eye level. This will help the person to feel more in control of the situation.
- Use physical contact to communicate your interest and to provide reassurance – don't underestimate the reassurance you can give by holding the person's hand or putting your arm around them, if it feels appropriate.

Speak Fluent Body Language

One of the benefits of becoming more aware of and 'reading' other people's non-verbal communication is that you become more aware of your own. It's likely you've not given much thought to whether your non-verbal communication helps or hinders your ability to communicate and connect with other people. In any one situation you're probably unaware how much you are conveying non-verbally, but you're no different from the rest of us; your body language and tone of voice can confirm, exaggerate, understate, or contradict what you say. You may, for example, say sorry but your tone and body language could be communicating your frustration and annoyance!

Other people draw conclusions about your attitude and intentions and, when faced with mixed messages, either they focus on your non-verbal messages or your mixed messages create confusion and distrust for the other person. So aim to avoid sending mixed messages; make your words, gestures, facial expressions, and tone match.

Top Tip

Say what you mean and mean what you say. Verbal and non-verbal messages are co-expressive – if you say what you mean, your body language will follow.

Confident Body Language

If there's a particular situation where you want to feel more confident, not just *appear* confident but genuinely feel confident about what you're saying, there's no need to adopt a range of poses, gestures, and expressions that feel unnatural to you. Instead, you simply need to adopt a couple of gestures or expressions and the rest of your body and mind will match up.

So, simply choose to do just two or three of these actions:

- stand or sit straight;
- keep your head level;
- relax your shoulders;
- spread your weight evenly on both legs;
- when you are sitting, keep your elbows on the arms of your chair (rather than tightly against your sides);
- make appropriate eye contact;
- lower the pitch of your voice;
- speak more slowly;
- speak more quietly.

You can't control every aspect of your non-verbal communication; in fact the harder you try, the more unnatural you will appear. But if you can just use one or two of those things consistently, your thoughts, feelings, and the rest of your behaviour will follow. It's a dynamic process where small changes in how you use your body can add up to a big change in how you feel, how you come across, and how you interact with other people.

Which two non-verbal behaviours would you feel comfortable using? Choose two and practise using them in a variety of situations.

In a nutshell

- What a person doesn't say – their non-verbal communication – can emphasize and support what they are saying. It can also contradict what they're saying.
- You can't rely on a *single* gesture, facial expression, and so on to confirm what someone does or doesn't mean or what they're feeling.
- You need to take a *combination* of non-verbal signals into consideration. Look out for a number of signs that all seem to add up to be 'saying' one thing.
- When you think that someone isn't coming across as honest or 'real' it's probably because their non-verbal communication doesn't match what they're saying. This mismatch creates a sense of confusion and distrust.
- A mismatch is known as 'leakage'. Leakage occurs when a person says one thing but their body language, gestures, and so on leak something different.
- Pay attention to changes in body language. Every shift in a person's emotions and feelings comes out in their non-verbal behaviour.
- Keep in mind that each person has their own particular style of gestures, facial expressions, ways of talking etc, called baseline behaviours. Be aware of what is 'in character' for someone and what is unusual for them.

- Don't over-analyse the other person's body language; and don't always assume you've correctly interpreted their non-verbal communication; remember to listen and ask questions!
- You're no different from the rest of us; your body language and tone of voice can confirm, exaggerate, understate, or contradict what you say. Aim to avoid sending mixed messages; make your words, gestures, facial expressions, and tone match.
- If there's a particular situation where you want to feel more confident, you simply need to adopt a couple of gestures or expressions and the rest of your body and mind will match up.

Part 2
Connect

6
Making Friends

Whether it's just a minute waiting for an elevator with a colleague or a few hours sat next to a friend's cousin at a wedding, with some people you feel comfortable talking to them and conversation just seems to flow quite naturally. But with others, it's not so easy; trying to engage the other person is like pushing a piano uphill; it's hard work. What to say? What to ask? How to respond? What if there's an awkward silence?

Small talk can be a big challenge. It doesn't come easily to all of us. It can be difficult enough to screw up your courage and initiate small talk, let alone keep a conversation going.

Perhaps you worry that you'll come across as weird or dull and the other person won't want to engage with you. But maybe you're not concerned with how you come across, it's more that you think small talk is shallow or boring; that it feels fake and a waste of time and that there's more to life than talking about the weather or the price of fish. Maybe so. But small talk can (although it doesn't have to) lead to big things! Sure, it might start with the obvious comments and pleasant exchanges but small talk serves an important purpose – it establishes the foundation for conversations in which interesting views, experiences, and ideas can be exchanged.

How to Make Small Talk

With small talk, it's simply about connecting; to come across as an approachable, friendly person who is open to exchanging a few pleasantries. You don't have to impress, you don't have to be brilliant. You just have to be nice. Smile, ask questions, listen, take a genuine interest in the other person, and say something about yourself.

Make the first move. Initiating conversation is a bold step; fear of rejection will be the main reason why people don't make the first move. If you're at a party, convention, or any other social gathering, choose a person who seems approachable; someone standing by themselves is a good bet, then just smile and say, 'Hi, I'm... What's your name?'

Get a grip. A handshake as limp as a wet noodle gives a poor first impression. If you're going to shake hands when you meet someone, extend your hand and give a warm handshake. Hold it for a beat as you look them straight in the eye, smile, and say hello. This is a simple and easy thing to rehearse with a friend. Practise until they feel that you've got it right. Then you'll have the right handshake for every situation.

Be positive. Don't start off with a moan or a complaint; say something positive.

Don't worry about coming up with clever conversation starters or having the 'right' thing to say. It doesn't matter if you make the usual comments: 'It's so cold today!' or questions: 'How do you know Sanjay?' or 'Have you been here before?' or 'What do you do/where do you work?' but you do need to be interested in and follow up on their answers.

Show an interest in the other person, their world, and what they might be interested in. Ask them about something that you notice about them. 'I see you came by bike. Do you do a lot of cycling?'

If it's appropriate, give them a sincere compliment – for example – 'I love your shoes! Where are they from?'

Comment or ask their opinion on something that both you and the other person are experiencing; where you're both at and what's around you. For example, say 'I really love this restaurant'. It's likely they'll ask you why, which opens up another opportunity for conversation. And if they don't, ask what they think of the place.

Be bold. Just about anything you find curious or interesting can start a conversation and keep things rolling. Maybe you read or heard about something interesting, something useful in the last few days. Maybe you heard an interesting theory? Tell them and then ask their opinion about it.

You can draw on stories from anywhere, from stories that happened to people you know, to those you came across in the news, the radio, a podcast, TV, magazines, and so on. If they stuck in your mind they must have been interesting to you. So they're good to share as just that: something that struck you as interesting, strange, or funny. Tell it, and then ask their opinion.

Ask for advice. As the nineteenth-century writer Arthur Helps observed, 'We all admire the wisdom of those who come to us for advice.' Using conversation openers that acknowledge the other person's skills or knowledge, such as 'You know a lot about travelling in France, don't you? What do you think would be the best way to get to Bordeaux from Nimes?' or 'You go to Glastonbury each year – where's the best area to camp?' is a good way to connect and get a conversation going. You learn something new and the other person gets to feel included and their expertise is acknowledged. (But don't ask someone for their professional advice at a social event. For example, at your cousin's wedding, don't ask another guest who's a doctor what they think about the rash on your leg!)

Top Tip

Still feeling apprehensive? Imagine that the other person is already your friend. You know a friend would respond positively if you approached them so pretend this person is already a friend.

Don't worry if you forget a name. It will help you to remember a person's name later in the conversation if you repeat their name when you are introduced to them: 'Nice to meet you, Madonna.' If you later find that you've forgotten her name, admit it. 'Gosh, I'm sorry, can you remind me of your name?' Once they've told you, don't make a big deal of it, simply repeat their name and move on with the conversation. 'Madonna. Thanks. Well, as I was saying...' It won't be nearly as tough as you think!

Make it easy for people to be introduced to each other. When you introduce one person to another, as well as telling each person the other's name, say something about each person. For example: 'Donald, this is Theresa. Theresa and her husband just moved here from London. Theresa used to work in government. Theresa, this is Donald. He's got an interesting theory on global warming which you might be interested to hear about.'

Ask questions. After the first few exchanges between you, you can keep the conversation flowing by asking more questions. Ask open questions that require more than a 'yes' or 'no' answer and give the other person an opportunity to talk about themselves, their opinions, or experiences. Good questions involve asking someone what they think or how they feel about whatever it is they're talking about. Even simple things like 'What was that like?' or 'How did it feel?' can keep people talking.

Top Tip

When someone tells you about something they've been doing or experienced, ask them; 'What was the best thing about it?' and 'What was the worst thing about it?' 'Why?'

If you've listened well, you can use any unexplored topics touched on earlier in the conversation to keep things moving. For instance, you might say, 'Earlier, you mentioned... can you tell me more about that?'

And if you've met and talked to someone before, try to remember something about them that you can ask them about, something they mentioned before. They might, for example, have told you about something that was currently happening in their life or that they were planning on doing. Ask them how things turned out. 'Last time we met you were training to be a driving instructor. How's that been going?'

Here are some more ideas for questions you can ask to start a conversation or keep it going:

Work

- What was your first ever job?
- What was the best or worst job you've ever had? Why?
- If you weren't working here, were would you like to be working? Why?

- Would you rather work four 10-hour days or five eight-hour days? Why?
- When you were a child, what did you think you were going to do when you grew up – was it this job?

Entertainment

- If you could only watch one genre of movies/read one genre of books for the rest of your life, what would it be? Why?
- Who are your favourite film stars/solo artists/bands? Why? What do you like about them?
- What was the last good book you read? What was the last good TV show or series you watched?

Food

- If you could only eat three things for the rest of your life, what would they be? Why?
- What's the weirdest thing you've ever eaten?
- What are your favourite comfort foods? Why?

Travel

- If you could fly and stay anywhere for free, where would you go? Why?
- What's the best and worst holiday you've been on? Why?
- If you could take six months' paid leave where would you go and what would you do? Why?
- Have you ever done a road trip? Do tell me about it.
- Where's the last place you travelled to? What did you do there?
- Do you prefer city or beach holidays? Why?
- What's the next trip you have planned?

Random Questions

- What would be your ideal superpower? Invisibility? To be able to fly? To breathe underwater? To see in the dark? To be able to read minds? Omnilinguilism? (the ability to speak any language) Atmokinesis? (the ability to control the weather)
- What talent or skill would you like to have – to sing, play a musical instrument, play a sport, draw, or paint?
- If you could have any type of animal for a pet, what would it be? Why?
- Are there any apps on your phone that you can't live without? (Last year, at a party, someone asked me this question and I explained that twice a year I lead walking holidays in Europe and that I couldn't live without the map app that I use. The other person was interested and asked me all about it. Our conversation led to him contacting the organization I work for and going on to become a walk leader himself!)

The greatest compliment that was ever paid me was when one asked me what I thought, and attended to my answer.

Henry David Thoreau

Listen for something in the other person's reply that might suggest a direction for the conversation to take. Follow up on what the other person says. Ask 'How come?' 'Why's that?' 'Why not?' 'What was that like?' Ask questions and, more importantly, listen and respond to the answers.

The next step is to draw on your own experience or knowledge of what the other person is talking about without taking over the conversation and turning it into being all about you! Communication is an exchange of thoughts, ideas, opinions etc. A conversation is like a jam session in jazz, where one starts with conventional elements and then spontaneous variations occur that take things in a new direction.

Top Tip

Remember, don't be afraid to ask questions if you're unsure or not clear about something the other person is telling you. Asking questions does not make you look stupid. You just need to listen to news programmes and chat shows on the radio and TV to know this; note how often the interviewer asks questions to clarify both their own and the listeners' or viewers' understanding.

Say Something about Yourself; Your Ideas, Experiences, Opinions

Although you might be genuinely interested in what the other person has to say, if you keep firing out questions the other person will feel that they're being interrogated! 'How do you know Rob?' 'What do you do?' 'Where do you work?' 'Where are you from?' 'Where do you live now?' That's too many questions in one go.

If you're talking to someone new and you've been asking them about themselves, at some point, you must say something about yourself. Maybe, though, you hesitate to talk about yourself; you're not comfortable with opening up and you find it easier to let the other person talk about themselves. But remember, communication is a two-way process – it involves an *exchange* of ideas, information, feelings etc, so you'll need to make a contribution yourself. Be willing to share a bit of yourself; who you are, your likes and dislikes, what you find interesting etc.

Did you lose your keys today or find £10? Tell the other person then ask if they've ever done the same. You could say something about a book you're reading, or an app you've found useful. What about a film, TV show, or box set you've recently watched? Tell the other person and ask if they've read, watched, or seen something good recently. Maybe you ate at a new restaurant last week, or heard some great new music. Tell the other person then ask if they've had a similar experience.

Top Tip

If you tend to speed up when you're nervous, excited, or stressed, or you use a lot of filler words – 'um's' and 'ers' – remember that well-placed pauses can make you sound and feel calm and collected. It will also make it more likely that the other person can follow what you're saying.

Often, awkward silences appear in conversation because you are worried about saying the 'right' thing and you hold back from saying something because you're not sure if it's clever or interesting enough. What does that do to the potential for conversation? It kills it!

Just say whatever comes to your mind. No asking yourself 'What would they think if I say this?' None of that. Say it. Then ask them what they think. If you feel like talking about the pizza you had for breakfast, do that. If you follow it up with a question 'What's the weirdest thing you've had for breakfast?' you've opened up the conversation. You'll discover that it's actually fine to let go and talk about whatever you feel like.

As my niece Olivia – one of the most likeable, friendly, fun people I know – says; 'You can always think of something – say what comes into your head and then see how the other person responds. Then take it from there.'

Keep the Conversation Going

When the other person asks you a question, respond with more than the minimum; give the other person something to pick up on. Here are some examples:

Question: 'How are you?'
   Short response: 'Fine.'
   Response that leads to further conversation: 'Good, thanks. I'm looking forward to next week – I'm going on holiday to Italy.'

Question: 'Where are you from?'
  Short response: 'Brighton.'
  Response that leads to further conversation: 'I'm from Brighton. Have you ever been to Brighton? You have? What did you like about it?'
Question: 'What did you do this weekend?'
  Short response: 'I went house-hunting.'
  Response that leads to further conversation: 'I went house-hunting. We're thinking about moving out to the country.'

Talking about yourself and sharing your thoughts and opinions doesn't mean you should monopolize conversations though. Be careful not to pontificate or lecture others on a cause or issue you care about. Over-explaining – sharing too much information, being too open, and boring people with unnecessary details – can quickly turn someone else's initial interest into agony as they're dying for you to stop and they tell themselves to avoid you next time!

The Traffic Light Rule

Ever listen to someone who, long after you've tuned out, continued to blab on? What did you think of that person? Probably that they were self-absorbed and unaware that you were losing interest or bored senseless. Without realizing it, could you be one of those people? Once you're on a roll, you may not even realize that the other person is trying to get a word in, or trying to cut things short. US author and career coach

---

Marty Nemko has some interesting advice for knowing how long is appropriate to continue talking: the traffic light rule for talking.

He suggests that in the first 20 seconds of talking, as long as what you're saying is relevant and appropriate, you're at a green light. When the light turns amber, you've moved into the next 20 seconds and you risk the other person being distracted or losing interest and tuning out. Once you've been talking for 40 seconds, your light is red. Yes, there's an occasional time you want to run that red light and keep talking – when the listener is obviously engaged – but the majority of the time, you'd better stop or you're in danger. You need to allow the other person a chance to say something or to ask a question.

Of course, it would be weird if you timed yourself each time you spoke. But Marty Nemko's advice can at least make you more aware of whether or not you have a tendency to waffle on too often!

Be sensitive to other's reactions to what you're saying. Look for clues; the other person's facial expressions and body language will tell you how they're feeling about what you're saying. If the other person is showing signs of being uncomfortable or disinterested – constantly breaking eye contact or glazing over, trying to interrupt you, fidgeting, frequently saying 'Yes', 'uh-huh', or 'right' as if urging you to get on with it – you're talking for too long. So wrap up what you're talking about, change the subject, and/or ask them a question.

Top Tip

The longer you talk, the more you need to be aware of the other person's responses, both verbal and non-verbal. Does your listener seem fully engaged? Whoever you're talking to – one person or several – keep an eye on their body language.

Top Tip

Learn what interest and boredom look like. Watch other people talking to one another in bars and cafes. Look for the signs that one person is or isn't interested in what the other person is saying. How can you tell?

Don't panic when there's a lull in the conversation. Think of silence as a transition. Either or both of you may need time to gather your thoughts. Don't feel the need to rush in and fill the void. Sometimes silence is appropriate. You don't want to seem like a babbling idiot! Often, the other person will start talking.

Otherwise, take the conversation in a new direction. Throw something out there; just choose any one of the questions or topics of conversation described in the last few pages and don't worry about making the transition smooth.

But if you do sense that the other person wants to get away, give them the opportunity to do so. For example, at a social event, you might say… 'I expect you want to talk to some others – I'm going to the loo – maybe chat again later.'

Finally, know when to stop and pull out. If the conversation feels like climbing a hill of sand then it may be time to move on or let silence take over. You can't connect with everyone, and some conversations simply refuse to take life!… Either way, end the conversation with something nice. For example, 'It was nice talking to you' or 'Have a good evening'.

Top Tip

Lose the phone. A 2014 study called *The iPhone Effect* demonstrated how the mere presence of a phone can ruin a conversation. The quality and substance of a conversation were rated as less fulfilling when compared to a conversation that took place in the absence of a mobile device. Leave it in your pocket or in your handbag and never place it on the table. And if you're expecting an important call or message, just let the other person know.

Build Your Confidence

If you want to feel more comfortable and confident about making small talk, you'll need to practise. Get into the habit of talking to people everywhere you go; challenge yourself to talk to an average of one new person a day, every day, for the next couple of weeks. At a shop, café, bar or restaurant, cinema or theatre, with anyone who works with the public, because they're used to people making small talk.

You could say something to a cashier in a supermarket. Look for a cashier who you can see chatting to a customer and so is open to remarks. 'It's quite busy/not very busy here today. Why's that do you think?' Or a charity collector – put some money in the collection tin and ask 'I expect you've been on your feet a long time already – how long will you be here today?' Acknowledge a neighbour and stop to exchange a few words. On the phone talking to someone at a call centre, ask what part of the country or what country they're speaking from. Ask what the weather is like there. At work, make a point of talking to someone you don't usually chat to. Talk to people who work in a different department from you.

Don't wait to feel confident about talking with other people before you start talking. The only way you'll feel more comfortable and confident talking to people is to do it frequently. What's the worst that can happen? Yes, you may be rebuffed or rejected, but feel the fear and do it anyway. By the time you've got over the fear, making small talk will be a habit. A good habit!

Do confident people ever feel anxious about communicating with other people? Yes, they do, but the difference between them and people lacking in confidence is that rather than focus on how much fear or anxiety they feel, confident people make use of their courage – they communicate with other people *despite* their trepidation. They recognize they have to start somewhere.

Talk to new people often enough and you'll eventually get comfortable making small talk and starting a conversation. Yes, it will feel strange and scary at first. And sometimes people will blank you. That's OK. They've got stuff going on and you don't know what it is. It's not you!

But after you've done this 10 times, 20 times, 30 times, it'll feel normal and natural. And who knows where it'll lead?

Put Yourself Out There

People tend to be a lot more open and talkative when they're doing something they're interested in or love doing. If you find people who are just as keen on, for example, board games or photography, wine tasting or Japanese cookery, hiking or singing as you are, then you'll have a much easier time making conversation and establishing connections.

Being with people who like the same things you do makes it easier for you to talk to them and make friends *because* you share similar interests and values. Go to www.meetup.com which will enable you to find and join groups of people in your local area who share your interests. There are groups to fit a wide range of interests and hobbies, plus others you'll never have thought of. There are book groups, art groups, film groups, and sci-fi groups. Gardening groups, singing groups, and cycling groups.

People who go to 'meetups' do so knowing they'll be meeting others who are also open to making new friends. If you find people who are just as keen on, for example, the theatre, gardening, politics, or craft beers as you are, then you'll find it relatively easy to connect and make friends with them. And when you're doing something that's fun and meaningful, your ability to form connections will feel natural.

You could also volunteer for a cause that you're interested in or that you feel strongly about. Go to do-it .org to find a wide range of volunteering opportunities near you. When you're involved doing something that you like and that has purpose and meaning for you, the opportunities to converse and to form connections will come more naturally.

How to Disconnect

How often have you found yourself stuck with someone who talks about topics in needless detail? Maybe they always bring the conversation back to themselves and don't ever ask you anything about yourself? They don't seem to understand that letting the other person talk, asking them questions and listening is an important part of being with other people. They're dull and boring but being polite and feigning interest will only encourage them to keep talking. Even worse, what if someone is being rude or offensive? If you don't want a confrontation, how do you cut them off and make a graceful exit? Here's how to do it:

Make contact. Take a deep breath and make eye contact. Say their name. If it's appropriate, briefly touch their arm. Stand up if you were sitting down.

Acknowledge what they've said. Rather than switch off, listen closely and use your listening skills to pick up and acknowledge something they said, then lead the topic to a close. 'So Paul, cycling from London to Paris was obviously quite a trip. I must do something like that myself one day.' Or 'Well Norman, you obviously feel strongly about immigration issues.'

Be nice. 'It was interesting hearing about your trip Paul, you've inspired me. Good to talk with you.'

You'll feel OK about ending the conversation and the windbag will be happier to let you go if you say something positive.

When someone is being offensive – in this example, Norman is making racist comments – if you feel that confronting them will only make them worse, take the high road and leave. Simply say, 'I don't agree with what you're saying – I find it offensive' and walk away.

Immediately explain your next move. After acknowledging, go straight into your next sentence. For example 'It was interesting hearing about your trip Paul, you've inspired me. Good to talk with you I need to go to the loo/call my babysitter/catch up with Alice.'

Note that there is no full stop between the words 'good to talk with you' and 'I need to...'. It's *crucial* that you don't pause between acknowledging what they've been talking about and announcing what you're doing next. If you don't pause they literally cannot get a word in edgeways.

Use the phrase 'I need': 'I need to get a drink/some food.' 'I need to talk to a client over there.' Do make sure you do what you say. Don't let the person see you were just making an excuse.

Widen the circle. Another way to disengage is to get other people involved. 'Paul do come with me, I want to introduce you to Alice/go to the bar/get some food.'

Whether the other person agrees to join you or not, this tactic makes the other person feel included, even if you then give him the slip. If you are already in a group and you want to stop the other person talking, try directing questions to someone else. Say: 'What do you think of this, Jessie?' Or 'I really want to hear what Fran says about this.'

Of course this all takes effort on your part, but these tactics will put you in control and taking control is better than being upset, offended, or bored senseless!

Getting Back on Speaking Terms with Someone Who's Giving You the Silent Treatment

Have you offended someone? Fallen out with a friend and now they're keeping their distance? Or maybe someone is giving you the cold shoulder and you don't know why?

Maybe it was something you said or something you did. Did you do something wrong or behave badly? Whatever the reason, by cutting you off the non-talker is trying to control the situation, protect themselves, or punish you. So how can you break through their wall of silence?

Fortunately, this is one of those situations where you can plan what you're going to say. Imagine you're alone with this person and say out loud what you want to say. Listen to the way you make your statement, and adjust your tone if need be. If the other person feels that you did do something wrong, you want to make sure your tone doesn't indicate that you think he or she is being over sensitive; a snide or patronizing tone will only make things worse between you. Positive body language is vital; folded arms, a tense posture, and avoiding eye contact is not going to demonstrate an honest open approach.

If you don't know what you've done wrong, say so. 'I feel like there's a problem between us and that you might be upset with me.' Ask what and how the other person is feeling. Do they feel hurt or frustrated? Maybe they simply feel let down. Try asking 'How do you feel about what happened between us'?

Listen and acknowledge what they say about how they feel. Explain how you feel, but be careful not to find fault or lay blame. Identify what you do and do not feel responsible for. Admit what, if anything, you could have done differently and that you're sorry it happened. Make it clear that you understand what you are apologizing for.

For example, 'I was angry and shouted – I'm sorry that upset you' or 'I didn't do what you asked me to do – I'm sorry I let you down.'

Ask what they think would help put things right between you. And explain what, if anything, you will do to put things right. You could, for example, say 'I know that when I get angry and shout, you don't get a chance to have your say. I know it's a bit late now, but please do tell me what you wanted to say.' Or, 'I know I let you down, I'd like to make up for it by...'

If you still cannot get through, you may have to find another way to communicate.

One way is to put it in writing. Again, take responsibility for what you could have done differently. Remember not to find fault or lay blame, but do acknowledge how you think the other person is feeling. Saying, for example, 'I can see that you are angry' shows that you are taking their feelings seriously. Explain how you feel and what you are willing to do to put things right.

Now it is up to the other person to step up and begin communicating with you.

If, despite all your attempts to break down the wall of silence, you cannot get through, you will know that you have tried your best and you just need to decide if you are willing to leave the door open for the other person to come through once they feel like talking again.

If, though, you're not prepared to wait, say something like; 'I'm upset that you're shutting me out and I wish you would talk to me so we can move forward. I'm finding it difficult to deal with so I'll have to stop waiting and just assume that you do not want to be friends anymore and we can leave it at that.'

In a nutshell

* Small talk is simply about connecting. You don't have to impress, you don't have to be brilliant. You just have to be nice. Smile, ask questions, listen, take a genuine interest in the other person and say something about yourself.
* Don't worry about having the 'right' thing to say. It doesn't matter if you make the usual comments or ask the usual questions but you do need to be interested in and follow up on their response.
* Keep the conversation going; draw on your own experience or knowledge of what the other person is talking about. Say something

---

about yourself; share your ideas, experiences, opinions.

- When the other person asks you a question, respond with more than the minimum; give the other person something to pick up on.
- Don't monopolize conversations though. Be sensitive to others' reactions to what you're saying. The other person's facial expressions and body language will tell you how they're feeling about what you're saying.
- If the conversation feels like climbing a hill of sand then it may be time to move on or let silence take over.
- Build your confidence. The only way you'll feel more comfortable and confident talking to people is to do it frequently. Yes, it will feel strange and scary at first. And sometimes people will blank you. That's OK. They've got stuff going on and you don't know what it is. It's not you.
- Put yourself out there. If you find people – through special interest groups or by volunteering – who are just as keen on or interested in the things as you are, the opportunities to converse and to form connections will come more naturally.
- Disconnecting from someone who won't stop talking or whose views you find offensive takes effort on your part. But putting in the effort and taking control is better than being upset, offended, or bored senseless!

- If someone is giving you the silent treatment and you don't know why, say so. Ask what and how the other person is feeling.
- Ask what they think would help put things right between you. And explain what, if anything, you will do to put things right. If you still cannot get through, you may have to find another way to communicate.

7
Supporting Others

If you're open, friendly, and show an interest in other people, they'll most likely want to talk with you; exchange ideas, thoughts and opinions, anecdotes and stories with you.

How, though, do you respond when someone is sad and upset, distressed, or depressed and struggling to cope? What to say when a family member, a friend, colleague, or your partner tells you that they're desperately unhappy and want to quit their job or their place at university? Or that they're very worried about their financial situation? How to respond to a colleague who tells you that his wife has left him? Or that their partner has been in a car accident or a close family member has been diagnosed with a serious illness?

There's not a lot you can say. At first, what's most important is that you listen; simply listen to what they're saying and feeling. Don't interrupt, don't try to fix it, pacify them, offer solutions, or stop their experience or expression of what they're thinking or feeling. You don't need to say anything, just being willing to listen can help a person feel less alone and isolated.

Be patient. You might want to ask questions and get more details about what's happened, and how they feel about it. But first, let the other person express themselves. Whatever they say, however long it takes them to tell you or however brief, when you think they've finished, count to three before you respond. This gives the other person an opportunity to continue, but it's not so long a pause that it appears you're not going to respond.

By giving them a chance to say what's happened and what they're feeling, by trying to understand what the other person is saying and feeling, you're being empathic.

If the other person has simply made a brief announcement you might need to know more. For example, someone might tell you that they're desperately unhappy in their job or on their university course. Simply ask them, 'Can you tell me more about that?' Other times, someone may have poured their heart out and given you a detailed description of their situation. In that case, you might start by clarifying and confirming what you've understood. Just say, 'So, can I just be clear, you're saying that... have I got that right?'

What to Say? Dos and Don'ts

Do ask about how someone feels about what's happened; 'How'd you feel about that?' Even if you think you know, let them tell you.

Don't say 'I know how you feel.' You don't need to have experienced the same situation as they have, you don't have to agree that you'd feel the same way in the same situation, you just need to have empathy; to recognize the other person's feelings and emotions and realize that, to a greater or lesser extent, they're having a hard time.

Do say something like 'I'm sorry that happened. It must be hard/confusing/ annoying/disappointing/upsetting for you.' In this way, you're validating that whatever it is, you understand that for them, it is hard, difficult, upsetting, or confusing or whatever it is they could be feeling. The other person might agree or they might disagree and explain further. For example, saying to someone whose elderly parent has recently died, 'You must be so upset' might be met with. 'No, actually, I'm very relieved. Mum had been ill for so long, it's a relief that it's now all over.'

Do ask open questions to encourage the other person to talk; to express their thoughts and feelings. Open questions that begin with What, Why, How, Tell me, Explain. For example; 'How did it happen?' or 'Why do you think he said that?' Don't interrogate them though.

Questions that Make a Difference

On 31 January 2019 @joannechodgetts posted this Tweet.

This morning, a junior doctor on the ward, her opening sentence to me & my husband; 'What do you understand to be happening?' Her closing sentence: 'Is there anything else you want to ask me?'

I wanted to hug her. ❤ *#HaveTheConversation*

More than 50 people tweeted a reply. Here's a few of them:

- Such a simple few words that can make a world of difference to a person's experience
- Two absolutely vital open-ended questions
- Great way to start and wrap up a dialogue with patients and family! Well done her
- So so important, when you are feeling nervous or worried, questions can be hard to vocalize. A friendly voice is so so important

Joanne responded by tweeting *'I'm going to show her (the doctor) this thread next week when she's back on duty, so she never forgets the impact of her words.'*

Don't think you can make someone to talk to you. It can take time for someone to feel able to talk openly, and putting pressure on them to talk might dissuade them from saying anything at all.

Do try and stay calm. Even though someone else's distress might be upsetting, try to stay calm. This will help the other person feel calmer too, and let them feel that they can talk freely, without upsetting you.

Don't give your thoughtful analysis of what went wrong and why. When your friend is turned down for a job or place on the course, or your sister's husband leaves her, someone tells you they've had a terrible day at work, or had a row with their partner, parent, or teenager your perspective might be useful but don't assume that you know how they feel or what will help.

Sometimes solutions are unnecessary, so don't feel you have to provide one. You may feel powerless about not being able to offer some practical help so don't suggest a juice fast, or that they need to meditate, or that you'll lend them that brilliant self-help book about being happier every day. Not now. Just listen. They may well appreciate you just listening more than your advice. (There's more on how to offer advice later in this chapter.)

Do be willing to sit in silence. Often, comfort comes from simply being in your company.

Don't say, if someone is going through a relationship break-up 'I never did like them' or 'You're better off without them'. They're probably already going over decisions they could have made differently, or signs they should have been looking out for. They don't need your disapproval, even if in your head it sounds like support.

Don't slip into clichés. It's easy to give unhelpful platitudes that offer no comfort but just irritate the other person. Don't say things like:

- Everything happens for a reason
- God never gives you more than you can handle
- It was meant to be
- It was not meant to be
- He's just gone to the next journey of his new life now
- It could be worse
- What's done is done
- Time is a great healer
- You need to put this behind you
- You'll get over it
- Think positive
- There's always someone worse off than you are

Do say. 'I'm sorry you're going through this' or 'I'm so sorry this has happened'.

Do suggest a walk or a drive. Sometimes it's easier to talk things through when you're both moving. The simple action of moving forward helps a person's mind to move forward, too. If someone is struggling to find a solution to a problem – feeling stuck in their job or a relationship – a walk in the park or countryside or a drive really can help open perspective and move things forward.

How to start a conversation with someone whose well-being you're concerned about

Samaritans (www.samaritans.org) – an organization that provides emotional support to anyone in emotional distress, who is struggling to cope, or is at risk of suicide – suggests that if you're worried about someone and don't know how to approach them about it, there are some things you can do to help them open up.

Often, people want to talk, but wait until someone asks how they are. Samaritans suggest that you gently try asking open questions like 'What happened about...', 'Tell me about...', 'How do you feel about...'. Unlike closed questions that just get a 'yes' or 'no' answer, asking open questions can help someone talk through their situation.

When – 'When did you realize?'
Where – 'Where did that happen?'
What – 'What else happened?'
How – 'How did that feel?'

Be an active listener; ask follow-up questions and repeat back the key things the other person has told you, using phrases like 'So you're saying...', 'So you think... is that right?'

If you say the wrong thing, don't panic. Samaritans say that there is no perfect way to handle a difficult conversation, so don't be too hard on yourself if it didn't go as well as you had hoped. If you feel able to, you might say something like 'Last week I said... and now I realize... and I'm sorry.'

Giving Bad News

Breaking bad news can be difficult and distressing for both giver and receiver. There are, though, ways to do it sensitively; with kindness and compassion. What matters most is how well you listen and how you respond to the other person's reaction.

Prepare for the conversation. If you can, think about what you're going to say. Anticipate their reaction and anticipate your reaction to their reaction. As well as thinking about what you're going to say, think about where you'll say it. Make sure to deliver the news in a place that is private, minimizes embarrassment, and allows the other person to maintain their dignity. But at the same time, think about your own safety and well-being because conversation can get heated and emotional. Sometimes people receiving negative news feel it's unfair. They want to fight back and argue.

Lay it out plainly. The other person needs to be clear about the situation. Here are two examples:

'Hello Lou. Thanks for coming to the interview. I'm afraid it's not the news you were hoping for; we've given the position to another candidate. (Pause) I can though, give you some feedback; tell you what you did well and give you some suggestions that might be helpful for interviews in the future.'

'It's not good news. (Pause) I'm afraid your lovely cat Bingo didn't make it after the operation. He died at 3 o'clock this afternoon. (Pause) He was old and just not strong enough. (Pause) He wasn't by himself; the nurse was with him. I'm sorry.'

Give reasons. Be prepared to explain why something happened and what caused it to happen, but do avoid lengthy explanations.

Anticipate questions and be prepared with concise and credible answers. If you don't have the answers, say so. If you know where the other person can get further information that might help to answer their questions, say so. If they have a question that's complicated, rephrase it to clarify it, but without changing the meaning. If it's angry, recast it in neutral language. Try and keep calm enough to answer the other person's questions with respect and sensitivity.

You may have been told that the best way to give bad news is to say something positive before and/or after the bad news. This is not to imply that things don't seem so bad, and certainly not to trivialize the bad news. The reason to include something positive is so that the other person has something positive to focus on. (As in the examples above 'I can give you some feedback; tell you what you did well and give you some suggestions that might be helpful for interviews in the future' and 'Bingo wasn't by himself; the nurse was with him.'

Bad news is usually met with strong emotions. Acknowledge those emotions but try not to get emotional yourself (unless the bad news directly affects you, too). Supposing, for example, you had to dismiss an employee. You can't *not* dismiss them because they're crying. But you can acknowledge their distress: 'I'm sorry you're so upset. I can see this has come as a shock' or 'I can see this is painful for you.' An empathic response acknowledges not only someone's feelings but also the reasons for those feelings.

Listen to the other person; let him or her talk. Validate their emotions, but primarily listen and acknowledge. Avoid saying 'I know just how you feel' or 'Try not to worry about it.' Although you might mean well, the other person might feel that you don't understand or you're attempting to bring things to a close.

If it's relevant, state what, if anything, you can do to help, or ask 'Is there anything I can do?' Avoid over-apologizing. Instead, suggest possible actions. No one wants excuses – they want a solution, direction, or tips on how to improve a situation or ideas for the future. Focus on what can be done rather than what can't be done.

Should you always deliver bad news in person? It may seem easier to convey bad news via text, email, or letter.

Certainly, you can plan exactly what to say and how to word it. You can also say what you want to without being interrupted. But you can't see how the other person feels and responds. And if that's the reason for putting it in writing, you've taken the coward's way out; you don't have to deal with the other person's response. Have courage! When you deliver difficult news in person, you can read the other person's body language and make appropriate adjustments in what you're saying. And you can clarify misunderstandings. So when you can, talk to the other person, face to face.

Giving Advice and Information

Whatever it is that someone else is upset or distressed about, listening is important, not just so that the other person can express themselves, but also because if the other person does want your opinion or advice, because you have listened and checked your understanding of their situation, what you say is more likely to be relevant and appropriate.

Giving advice can provide new ideas and information, and help the other person identify their options, make a decision, move forward, and feel more in control. So, having listened and clarified your understanding of their situation, if you feel you have something to say that could help, if they haven't said so already, ask them 'What do you want to happen?' so that you can relate your advice directly to what they do or don't want to happen.

To make sure your advice is well received, bear in mind the following:

- **Ask.** 'Do you want some ideas to improve the situation?' or 'Can I suggest something?' or 'Can I give you my opinion/advice?' And if you've had a similar experience or know of someone else who has, just say 'That's happened to me/happened to my friend. Let me know if you think it would be helpful for you to hear about it.' If, for example, someone confided in you about a health problem they had that you had also experienced, the other person's thoughts and feelings about their situation might be different to yours, but by sharing your own experience, they might pick up some insights rather than feel they'd been *told* what to do.
- **Be positive.** Rather than start your advice with, 'Why didn't you...?' or 'You should have...' accept what's done is done, and focus on what they can do next. Say something like, 'How about...?' or 'It might help to consider...' or 'Perhaps you could try...'
- **Keep your advice short and to the point.** Whenever you've talked for a minute or so, bring it back to them. 'What are your thoughts about that?'
- **Know when to let go.** There are no magic words that will make everything OK. Even if the other person asks for your advice, they won't necessarily take it. The best you can do is listen, validate feelings, and support them in whatever way you're able to. It's important to accept that there are always limits to what you can say and do to

support someone else. They may need professional help. Depending on what the issue is, you can help them to find out more from an organization that helps people cope with a specific problem such as, for example, the mental health organization MIND www.mind.org.uk or nationalbullyinghelpline.co .uk or samaritans.org or ageuk.org.uk or citizensadvice.org.uk. Simply Google the issue – 'mental health support', for example, or 'cancer support' or 'debt advice' and there will most likely be an organization that can give expert advice.

Encouragement, Compliments, and Praise

Listening, offering advice, and encouragement could motivate someone to take a brave step, persist with and complete a difficult task, say 'no' to an unnecessary obligation, or do something that they didn't feel strong enough to do before.

When you see someone making progress, no matter how small, say something; give a compliment or praise. Acknowledge their efforts and point out what they're achieving. If an encouraging thought comes to mind, share it! Don't hold back. Tell them face to face, by text, or email.

In fact, giving encouragement to someone else doesn't have to be just for times when they're struggling.

There are many reasons you might encourage someone with a compliment or praise – it could be they've achieved or overcome something, made a special effort, or put extra time into something that has benefited you or someone else. So tell them! You don't need to worry about getting the wording just right. A genuine sentiment phrased a bit awkwardly is better than saying nothing at all. And anyway, your body language, tone of voice, and facial expressions will show that your compliment or appreciation is genuine.

Start with the reason why you're praising the other person. Be specific. Sometimes the most memorable compliments are the most specific ones, because it shows that you noticed. For example;

'You've done so well, coping throughout your partner's illness.'

'You handled that rude customer so well. Well done for being so patient with him.'

Acknowledge personal qualities or special efforts; a person's concern and patience or the extra time they put into something. Notice when someone has managed a personal difficulty. Notice the work someone does. It could be someone who serves you in a shop or café, it could be something about someone's business or someone in your office. Make a positive comment about their work or business. Even if what they did is their duty or a part of their job, it doesn't mean they don't deserve to be appreciated for it.

If you like or admire something someone has done, achieved, or overcome, don't keep it to yourself. Tell them! Let the other person know that their efforts or actions have been noticed.

And if someone has done something that has had a direct impact on you, do be sure to give a sincere thank you. Let them know the difference their efforts have made; people feel good if they know that they made a positive difference, so as well as saying thanks, explain how. For example:

'Thanks for doing that; you saved me a lot of time.'
'Thank you for explaining that. You really helped me understand the situation more clearly.'

Finally, when it's appropriate, send a letter, card, text, or email expressing your appreciation. This shows thought on your part while also giving the person a permanent reminder of the praise.

In a nutshell

- When someone is struggling to cope, what's most important is that you listen; simply listen to what they're saying and feeling. Don't interrupt, don't try to fix it, pacify them, offer solutions, or stop their experience or expression of what they're thinking or feeling. You don't need to say anything, just being willing to listen can help a person feel less alone and isolated.
- Be patient. You might want to ask questions and get more details about what's happened,

and how they feel about it but first, let the other person express themselves.

- If the other person has simply made a brief announcement you might need to know more. Other times, if they've given you a detailed description of their situation, you might start by clarifying and confirming what you've understood.
- Do ask open questions to encourage the other person to talk; to express their thoughts and feelings. Ask how they feel about what's happened.
- Say something like 'I'm sorry that happened. It must be hard/confusing/annoying /disappointing/upsetting for you.' Do try and stay calm. Don't think you can make someone to talk to you; be willing to sit in silence.
- Don't feel you have to provide a solution or advice. Don't say you know how they feel or slip into clichés.
- There are ways to break bad news sensitively; with kindness and compassion. What matters most is how well you listen and how you respond to the other person's reaction.
- Prepare for the conversation: think about what you're going to say and what their reaction might be. Anticipate questions and be prepared with concise and credible answers. Include something positive so that the other person has something positive to focus on. Think about where you'll say it.

- When you can, talk to the other person, face to face. Get right to the point, explain the how and why, leave no room for misinterpretation, and be as calm and kind as you can.
- Listen to the other person; let him or her talk. Validate their emotions, but primarily listen and acknowledge.
- Focus on what can be done rather than what can't be done. Say what, if anything, you can do to help, or ask 'Is there anything I can do?'
- When you do give advice, keep it positive, short, and to the point. Whenever you've talked for a minute or so, bring it back to them. 'What are your thoughts about that?'
- Know when to let go. Even if the other person asks for your advice, they won't necessarily take it. The best you can do is listen, validate feelings, and support them in whatever way you're able to. Accept that there are always limits to what you can say and do to support someone else. They may need professional help.
- When you see someone making progress, no matter how small, say something encouraging; give a compliment or praise. Acknowledge their efforts and point out what they're achieving.
- Giving encouragement to someone else doesn't have to be just for times when they're struggling. If you like or admire something someone has done, achieved, or overcome, don't keep it to yourself; let the other person know that their efforts or actions have been noticed.

- And if someone has done something that has had a direct impact on you, do be sure to give a sincere thank you.
- When it's appropriate, put it in writing. This shows thought on your part while also giving the person a permanent reminder of the praise.

8
Winning People Over With Persuasion

Set up the listening. Prepare who you are talking to for what you want them to hear. Get people to listen as a possibility rather than a problem.

Mal Pancoast

Whether you're hoping to persuade others to give you something you want or do things your way, or to help you with something, accept your suggestion, or agree with your point of view, most likely your intentions are good but, as is the case for many of us, your intentions are often let down by how and what you say. You hint and imply or berate and badger, beg, implore, or even insist. Certainly, you may get people to comply by making demands; but that's forcing people to do things in a way that works for *you* and probably only serves *your* interests. You may succeed in getting things done how you want, but you won't succeed in winning people over.

Persuading is a skill. There are better and worse ways of doing it.

Two thousand years ago, the Greek philosopher Aristotle suggested that there are three ways to persuade other people: through ethos, pathos, and logos.

Pathos involves appealing to people's emotions; emotions such as pity, anger or fear. It means convincing someone else by creating an emotional response; making an impassioned plea or telling an emotional story. A good example of this is a Telethon – a televised fundraising event – the purpose of which is to raise money for a worthy cause. By presenting emotional stories to appeal to your feelings, it hopes to persuade you to donate money to the cause.

Logos involves using logic and reason to persuade the other person. It may involve stating facts and figures, evidence and proof. For example, if someone was persuading you to invest a sum of money they might say: 'At the current rate of return, if you invest £500 now, you'll have £700 later this year.'

But as well as appealing to a person's sense of reason – logos – and to their feelings – pathos – the likelihood of successfully persuading someone to do something depends first and foremost on ethos. This means that whatever it is you're trying to persuade someone else to do, you first have to have their trust and respect; they have to see you as someone who has integrity. They have to believe that you have authority, knowledge, and experience of what you're talking about and hoping to persuade them to think or do. As Aristotle said: 'We believe good men more fully and more readily than others.'

People are much more likely to agree, do what's suggested or help out if they believe the other person is being sincere, decent and fair and doesn't have a hidden agenda. Think of a time that someone has persuaded you to do something – to take their recommendation or to do things differently or see things their way. Was it someone you disliked and distrusted? It's unlikely!

So, if you want to encourage and motivate, persuade and influence people to do something, you'll need to appeal to their heads and their hearts; you'll need to engage their logical, rational reasoning side and engage their emotions and imagination. And you'll need to be credible; believable and trustworthy.

Consider the Other Person

Assuming then, that your intentions are good and the other person likes and trusts you, there's a number of considerations that can help you engage them with logic and emotion. What do you already know about the other person that might help you to engage them? Are they more likely to engage in a conversation that takes place somewhere quiet with no distractions, or over a drink or a meal, or while doing an activity together? What's their communication style? Do you know if they're 'active', 'purposeful', or 'theoretical' communicators? (See Chapter 1.) If so, you may need to emphasize the logical, rational reasons for doing what you're asking them to do. If their communication style is more of a 'connector' they may be more easily persuaded if you appeal to their feelings.

What else do you already know about the other person that might help you to persuade them? You might, for example, know that rather than spend time with family, your teenager would rather spend time hanging out with their friends. You also know that they enjoy water sports. To persuade your teen to join you for a family holiday you might organize a holiday where they had access to water-based activities and/or you might offer for them to bring a friend on holiday.

Choose the right person. If, for example, you want to persuade someone to help you move furniture or help you with an IT problem, is there someone who is more likely to agree to help because they have the skills, knowledge, and time.

It is easier to persuade someone to do something if they've acted that way before. Supposing you want someone to help out with a fundraiser at work and you know that a particular colleague was recently involved in a charity challenge, it's likely you'll be able to persuade them to join you in the cause you are supporting. (Don't assume that this is definitely the case – they may have compassion fatigue!)

Be careful not to try and persuade the other person only according to what issues are important to you, not them. How might they feel about the issue or situation? What do they already know? What are *their* needs and interests and wants? If, for example, you know that two other people have successfully asked your manager to change their hours at work, find out what it was that persuaded him or her.

Letting People Make Their Own Decisions

In her book *In Shock: How Nearly Dying Made Me a Better Intensive Care Doctor* Rana Awdish explains the importance of not assuming you know what's best for someone else. She writes: 'As a physician, I had often entered rooms, believing that I knew what the right choice was and that I needed to make people agree with me. We were trained to believe that we had the answers, that we knew what was right, and we weren't trained to ask generous questions, to ask, "What would help you most with your healing right now? What do you feel would be useful to you?" We didn't have any sort of understanding that the patient is the holder of knowledge that is unique for them.'

When you're trying to persuade someone to do something, tell them how it will benefit them. For example, 'How about you cook dinner tonight, then I can finish this work, put the children to bed and that will leave enough time for us both to watch the film.' (Notice how, in this example, the words 'how about' create a suggestion. Very often, persuasion can be most effective if you use suggestion rather than demand.)

But if you're asking someone to help you out or do you a favour, again, don't assume that you know what incentives they will need. It could be different from what you think ought to be motivating to them, so ask questions. What reasons, what incentives, what rewards in return for their cooperation – their time and effort – would they like?

If you can give someone something, great. But if you can prevent something from being taken away, that can be even more persuasive. People may be more persuadable when they're confronted with loss, rather than gain. There's a story in which two groups of employees were presented with a proposal for an IT project. Twice as many of them were persuaded to approve the proposal if the company was predicted to lose £500,000 if the proposal wasn't accepted, compared with a scenario that predicted the project would lead to a profit of £500,000.

If you can help them avoid something that's stressful they may be more likely to say yes. Certainly point out what you think the result or outcome will be of not doing things the way you want, but don't use emotional blackmail or threats to describe what will happen if they don't do things your way!

Is there an option a and an option b you can offer? For example, to a small child: 'We need to go out in ten minutes. Do you want to wear your blue shoes or your red shoes?'

Whenever it's practically possible, choose a good time so you can persuade the other person when they are at their most responsive and open to considering what you want and what you're asking for. Don't try saying something when they're tired, stressed, or likely to be distracted.

Be Clear, Confident, and Honest

Once you've considered the other person's position, before you say anything, make sure you know what, exactly, it is that you want to persuade the other person to do. Keep it focused; simplify your request and don't ramble on, otherwise your message will be lost. Hit the headline first. For example, to your manager at work you would say: 'I'd like to change my work hours' and then explain how and why. And in another example to a friend whose welfare you're concerned about: 'I'm worried about you and I'd like you to get some help.' Then explain why you're worried, what help you think they might need, and where they could go to get that help.

Acknowledge – but don't make a big deal about – any practical or emotional gain you stand to receive should the other person agree to do what you've asked. For example, to your friend whose help you need you might say: 'If you could help me move into my new flat, it would save me the money of hiring a removal firm. And with all the other moving costs, that would save me quite a bit.' And to your teenager, you might say: 'I'd be really pleased if you joined us and we were all together for this holiday. It'd make me happy having all the family together.'

Explain how you feel about the issue. Persuasion requires and involves emotion, but don't let feelings take over. Acknowledge – but don't make a big deal about – what you stand to lose. Be honest; explain what's at stake for you; what you're concerned about. If you were someone hoping to change your work arrangements, you might say: 'If I can't work from home two days a week, I'm not sure how I'll be able to manage childcare. I'm worried I won't be able to continue with the job.' And to a friend who you were trying to persuade to get some help: 'I'm concerned that if you don't go to the doctors and get it checked out, your condition will just get worse.'

Say what you're prepared to do towards it. People are more likely to help do something rather than do the whole thing. So if, for example, the laundry needed doing, you might say: 'I've sorted through the washing and put a white wash on. When it's finished, could you hang it all out to dry?'

Be aware of your body language. Assuming you're sincere and have good intentions, your body language should naturally reflect your sincerity and honesty. If you're nervous about asking the other person, remember to adopt two gestures that will help you feel and come across as confident and remember that you have a right to ask for what you want.

Listen, Acknowledge, and Clarify

Once you've told the other person what you want and briefly explained why, stop talking. Stop talking and listen to the response. If, after they've responded, you're not clear about what the other person does and doesn't want or how they feel about what you're suggesting, ask questions. People are more likely to cooperate if they feel acknowledged and understood. Are you clear about their concerns and objections? Acknowledge and address those objections.

Saskia is talking with her brother-in-law, Joe. She's heard of a job where she works that she thinks would be perfect for him. She tells him about it but he looks doubtful. 'The job sounds really interesting,' says Joe, 'but you said it involves a fair amount of travel to Europe. That wouldn't have been problem a couple of years ago but recently, two things happened. On a flight to New York last year, another passenger had a major panic attack just before we took off. They freaked out and it really unsettled me. Then, a few weeks ago on a flight to Italy, the plane I was on hit severe turbulence. It was terrifying. So now I'm nervous about flying.'

Saskia replies by saying: 'But, Joe, it's a really good job. I think it'd be just right for you – it's really well paid too. *And* I think I can probably get you on the inside track.'

Saskia has been listening to herself – what she has to offer – rather than listening to Joe's concerns. However, if she'd listened and acknowledged what Joe had told her, she might have said: 'Oh! Yes, both those situations sound like they were really scary – I can understand why you're apprehensive. Would you think about applying and at the same time getting some help to overcome your fear of flying?'

Listening with an Open Mind

Saskia would have been more helpful and made a better connection with Joe if she'd listened with an open mind. Listening with an open mind means being willing to listen to someone else's experience, their opinions and ideas, without making assumptions or jumping to conclusions. Our assumptions, beliefs, and judgements are often behind much of what we misinterpret and misunderstand. Assumptions and judgements, biases and prejudices can easily distort what the other person is saying to you.

Of course, the hardest time to listen with an open mind is when you are listening to something you don't want to hear. When, for example, someone is disagreeing with you or refusing to do what you want them to do. But open-minded listening doesn't mean you have to agree with what they're saying. You can listen to someone talking about their point of view about a political issue for example, without approving of their opinion. Of course, you may disagree, but because you listened, you know exactly what it is you are disagreeing with! Furthermore, if you listen with an open mind, you might learn something; something useful or interesting.

If there is any one secret of success, it lies in the ability to get the other person's point of view and see things from that person's angle as well as from your own.

Henry Ford

The Backfire Effect

In his book *The Intelligence Trap: Why smart people do stupid things and how to make wiser decisions*, David Robson explains that Sir Arthur Conan Doyle – the author of the Sherlock Homes books – frequently visited fraudulent mediums. His friend, the illusionist Harry Houdini, tried to persuade him that they were tricksters. But rather than accept his friend's advice, Conan Doyle decided that Houdini himself must be a paranormal being, who was lying to hide his own magical powers.

When you're hoping to persuade someone to do something, telling them that their opinion is wrong is unlikely to work; it will probably just make them defensive and even more unwilling to accept further evidence. One of the problems with arguing against someone else's way of seeing things is that it can result in what's known as 'the backfire effect'. The backfire effect occurs when evidence that contradicts a person's belief actually makes it stronger. Showing people evidence to prove that they are wrong can cause them to find a reason or reasons to support their original stance more strongly than they previously did. So, for example, presenting negative information about a political candidate that a person supports may cause them to find reasons to increase their support for that candidate.

> People who are convinced against their will, are of the same opinion still.
>
> Samuel Butler

If you're trying to explain to someone the issues with their stance, you can mitigate the backfire effect by presenting a different view in a way that encourages the other person to consider and accept that view, instead of rejecting it outright.

You need to explain things in a non-confrontational way, a way that allows people to consider a different opinion or view and reach the conclusion that you want them to reach themselves. One way to do this is by thinking about and including the counterarguments.

Dealing with Racist Remarks

Amnesty International's Australian website www .amnesty.org.au acknowledges that knowing how to respond to racist remarks can be a minefield. On the one hand, you want to call the other person out for their misinformed bigotry but doing so can lead to an argument or awkwardness, without actually convincing them to change their view. So how do you communicate clearly and effectively to help reduce the casual racist remarks others make? With suggestions from Sue Yorston, who manages Relationships Australia, Victoria's social inclusion portfolio, here's some of what Amnesty advise.

Rather than saying 'You're a racist', talk about how those comments are impacting you and how you are feeling about it.

Clarify their stance. One of the swiftest ways to an argument is mishearing or misunderstanding somebody's point. So if you've been shocked by what you perceive as a racist outburst, it could be worth getting them to articulate their perspective. 'Sometimes what we say and what we hear are two different things,' Sue points out. 'Somebody might say something and have a different intent and not realise what the impact is going to be.'

'You might not provide answers – you might be able to ask questions to help them challenge their own stereotypes.'

As tempting as it might be to call a racist out in front of a group, Sue says that sometimes you'll have a greater persuasive effect if you take them aside quietly later and highlight your concerns. 'You could say something like, "What you said before has been sitting with me and I want to talk to you about it",' she suggests. 'Often we make stereotypical racist-based comments from ignorance so it's an opportunity to educate and say, "Hang on a minute, that hasn't been my experience".'

Listen to their perspective. As abhorrent as their views might seem, if you don't give people the respect of listening to their views, then there is little chance that they'll do the same for you.

New US research suggests that 61% of conservatives and 64% of liberals prefer to read arguments they already agree with, which means a lot of arguments fall on deaf ears – on both sides of the political fence. 'Participants said that hearing from the other side felt lousy; they reported it was about as unpleasant as taking out the trash or standing in line for 20 minutes,' the psychology researchers from the Universities of Winnipeg and Chicago wrote.

But the researchers say that listening to both sides of an argument could help you get your point across. 'If their political opponents feel understood, they might be more receptive to hearing what others have to say,' they point out. 'Listening to the other side could at least help prepare an arsenal of counter-arguments.'

Think About the Counterargument

If you want to change someone's mind, you have to know what's important to that person. As certain as you are that your opinion is the right one, you need to be able to understand the other person's possible objections.

Marlene Caroselli

Consider the argument against what you're saying, asking, or suggesting. Though it may seem counterintuitive, you will be more persuasive if you acknowledge and address the opposing point of view. In fact, even before you talk to the other person, you can anticipate objections and concerns. Put yourself in the other person's place and imagine what their objections might be. Here are some examples:

- You can take part in the 10km run. *I know you think that you're not fit enough, there's only six weeks until the run and you think there's not enough time to get fit.* (The counterargument) I've thought about that and what we could do is...
- You should apply for the promotion. *It's true that you don't have enough experience for the role* (The counterargument) but you could explain in the interview that you're willing to shadow someone else on the job and put in the extra hours to come up to speed.
- You don't have to carry on doing this. *Yes, it may feel weak to have changed your mind.* (The counterargument) But instead of seeing it as a U-turn, see it as having made a new decision.

If people are unsure or resistant, find out what their feelings and concerns are. Persuading others often means that you acknowledge the difficulties but are clear that they *can* overcome difficulties and succeed. Be positive and optimistic. Acknowledge the challenges but emphasize the positive.

'You need to leave that job. That bullying colleague is persistently criticizing and humiliating you and they

155

won't stop. Staying there will make you ill. Put your energy into finding another job.'

Compare the effect of what was just said, with the following, which includes the counterargument that acknowledges the objection/opposing view. (In italics)

'You need to leave that job. *I know you think your bullying colleague can't really help it because they are stressed and finding it difficult to cope.* But they are persistently criticizing and humiliating you and they won't stop.

I can see that it would feel like the bully had won. But by leaving, you take away the opportunity for them to continue their behaviour towards you. *Of course, I realize that it means leaving a good job and financial stability*, but you'll also have left the bully behind. Once you left them, instead of trying to pacify or avoid the bully, you can put your energy into finding a new job.'

Steel-manning

Rather than directly argue your point and saying 'You're wrong. My way is right', acknowledging the counterargument can be a more effective way to persuade someone. Another, similar approach is known as 'steel-manning'. Steel-manning involves restating the other person's position clearly and fairly and then you move things on to another way of thinking.

You first explain that you understand what and why the other person thinks and feels as they do and that it's valid, and then you develop that thinking by taking it further in a way that suggests the next logical step. The other person sees you do understand their position, interests, and feelings. It also allows them to save face and not be seen to have backed down. They're not proven wrong, they just arrive at your point of view through extended thinking.

Suppose, for example, you were trying to persuade a relative that their health care needs would be better met in a care home. They might have said to you:

'I don't know if this is the right time. I've lived here for so many years – me and your Dad brought both you kids up here. I'm not completely incapacitated you know. I can still do some things for myself.'

Your reply could be 'Yes, it's been such a lovely family home, hasn't it? We've got lots of happy memories to look back on. I know you feel that you're not ready yet and you're certainly not helpless, that's for sure! I understand that you need to get to a point where you feel ready; being prepared is important. I agree...

(At this point you've explained that you understand what and why the other person thinks and feels as they do and acknowledged that it's valid. Next, you develop their thinking by taking it further in a way that appears to suggest the next logical step.)

'... and so if we start looking now, we can take our time exploring all the options and find the right place for you. And then, both of us know that if an emergency ever happened, we already have a plan for you to be in an environment that can meet whatever needs may then pop up. Otherwise, we might have to deal with a health setback and a move in quick succession, which is always physically and emotionally difficult. Moving sooner rather than later could avoid a great deal of stress down the road.'

So, with a steel-manning approach, when the other person has objections, don't just contradict them. Acknowledge that what they say is understandable; that their point of view is valid and why it's valid. And then explain how what you're saying leads on from what they're saying. It's an approach that accepts where they or the situation are at, but shows the road ahead.

A variation on this approach is to talk about what you used to believe, and what you believe now. Describe how you (or someone else you know) once felt the same as the other person does, then you describe how your mind (or someone else's) was changed, and what you instead found to be true. So if you want to change Uncle George's mind at the family dinner this weekend, if you can point out one part of his views that you agree with, he'll be more likely to consider your perspective.

Top Tip

Be inspiring; help the other person visualize what success will look and feel like. When you're inspiring people, you're aiming to engage their imaginations and emotions; to get them to feel and see what's possible. Aim to describe things in a way that will generate images in their minds that provide a clear picture of what can be achieved.

Top Tip

Be patient. Urgency and immediacy are often the enemies of persuasion. People are best brought on board in their own time. Make your suggestion and leave them to think about it. If circumstances allow, give people time to come round to your way of thinking. Allow time for ideas to settle in and for people to discover the logic in an argument.

Use Positive Language

Not only can you be more aware of how you structure and phrase what you say, but when you're hoping to persuade someone, you need to be more conscious about the words you use.

'And' not 'But'

Look at these two sentences:

'Thanks for doing the washing up as I asked. *But* you
haven't dried up.'
'I think your idea is great, *but* you should focus more on
meeting deadlines.'

'But' is a minimizing word that detracts from the positive thought or statement before it. In this example, by
using the word 'but' you've taken away from the fact
that the other person did, though, do the washing up. In
the case of the report, you've minimized the fact that the
report *has* been written. Replacing the word 'but' with
'and' creates and extends a much more positive meaning. By using the word 'and' you make it more likely that
the other person will be persuaded to do what you want
them to. 'But' is final. 'And' implies there's still more to
come, as you can read here.

'Thanks for doing the washing up *and* if you could
just dry the dishes and put them away, that'd be
great.'
'I think your idea is great, *and* if you could focus more
on meeting deadlines, things really will improve.'

Each time, the word *and* compels you to complete the
sentence in a positive way. If you turn back to page 158
you can see how using the word 'and' is effective when

using a 'steel-manning' approach. You'll see that the person positively phrases their relative's concerns and then seamlessly develops their thinking by using the word 'and' (not 'but') to suggest the next logical step.

'But' not 'And'

It works the other way round too; in different circumstances, replacing 'and' with 'but' makes a negative sentence more positive.

For example, 'You're so unfit *but* you can exercise and get fitter.' This sentence started out as a negative thought, then got turned into a positive thought.

This time the word 'but' encourages you to complete your sentence with something positive:

'I know you think you'll never find a partner *but* if you start going out more, you could meet someone.'
'It feels like we'll never pay off this debt…' becomes 'It feels like we'll never pay off this debt, *but* if we get some expert advice there could be a way to work it out.'

Should or Could?

Persuasion is often more effective if you use suggestion rather than demand. Instead of saying 'should' or 'shouldn't' try using 'could' instead. Using the word 'could' instead of 'should' suggests that there is in fact a choice of whether to do something or not. This shift in use of words is a more positive, flexible approach to thinking and doing things.

Rather than saying that someone should or shouldn't do something – which is demanding and creates pressure – by saying 'could' you're suggesting there's a choice about what to think and do or not think and do.

Top Tip

Listen to people talking on debate programmes on the TV and radio. Be aware of how and when other people use 'should', 'shouldn't', 'can't', 'must', and 'mustn't' when trying to persuade someone to see things from their point of view. Do they come across as persuasive or domineering? Listen out for other people's negative words and phrases and think of positive alternatives.

Never Ever and Always

Words like 'always' and 'never' are examples of 'all or nothing' thinking. They are words that are often unhelpful because the statements that include them are rarely true. For instance, 'You always avoid doing what I want' is probably not true. They don't *always* avoid doing what you want, do they? It would far more realistic to say 'You often...'.

Don't Do That!

Telling the other person what you do want rather than what you don't want to happen may increase your chances of a positive outcome... Tell them what you want them to do rather than what you don't want them to do. It's a far more positive message. Rather than saying, for example, 'Don't throw the ball inside!' Say 'Please take the ball outside.'

'Can' not 'can't'

Positive phrasing and language tells the other person what can be done rather than what can't be done. It sounds helpful and encouraging, suggests alternatives and choices, emphasizes positive actions and positive outcomes.

Even if the message you have to convey is negative, you can soften the impact by using the positive form of a sentence. For example, instead of saying 'You *can't* work on Project A' a more positive message is 'You *can* work on Project B.'

And, instead of 'I won't know until tomorrow' say 'I will know tomorrow.'

Use positive language. Talk about positive possibilities of doing things the way you're suggesting. Using words such as 'We will...' and 'You can...', 'I'll be able to' is much more open and helpful.

When you're trying to persuade someone, words and phrases such as 'You should', 'You ought to', 'You must', 'Unless you' are domineering and can imply a threat. Words that suggest fault – 'You haven't', 'You failed to' – and phrases that suggest the person isn't being honest – 'You claim that...' – limit the other person's willingness to accept your views or way of doing things. They are less likely to cooperate. Negative language is at best demotivating and uninspiring and at worst it can provoke refusal, hostility, and confrontation.

As well as having a negative effect on the other person, negative language doesn't help *you*, either. It restricts your thinking and demonstrates your bias. Avoid using absolute or extreme words. Rather than strengthening your message, extreme words like 'always', 'never', 'definitely', and 'absolutely' exaggerate, overstate, and can weaken the credibility of what you're saying.

Remember, your aim is to be understood and get someone to respond in the way you hope. Positive words and phrases make that more likely to happen. The same is true if you put it in writing.

Top Tip

Remember, if you're hoping to come across as confident, authoritative, or persuasive, um's, er's, and ah's will have the opposite effect; they'll undermine and weaken what you're saying. Replace fillers with pauses. Well-placed pauses can make you feel and sound calm and collected.

Persuading the Other Person to Negotiate

So often, when we're hoping to persuade someone to do or see something our way, either one or both of us stake out firm positions by stating our positions in absolute terms. We say things like 'I definitely will not/do not want...' or 'I totally refuse to', 'I absolutely cannot...', 'There's no way I can...', 'It's going to be impossible for me...', 'I'll never ...'. We set ourselves up for an impasse; a position from which there is no negotiation; deadlock. It doesn't have to be like this! The way forward is to identify and understand each other's position and interests. Doing this is a necessary stepping stone towards achieving a satisfactory outcome; one that satisfies both sides.

What's the difference between positions and interests? Your position is where you stand on an issue; your point of view. Your interests are the reasons why you think and feel that way; what's important or is of concern.

For example, Jim states his position by saying to his son: 'You are *definitely not* (an absolute term) going to stay out late on a school night. I am *not* going to allow it.'

Lee answers by stating his position: 'There is *no way* (an absolute term) I'm missing Jenna's party. I *am* going and I *will* be home late. And you're not going to stop me.'

A more constructive conversation could start like this;

> **Jim:** I don't want you staying out late on a school night. (Jim's position)
> **Lee:** I want to go to the party and stay till midnight, when it finishes. (Lee's position)

It would be easy for Jim to react to his son by repeating his position (I don't want you staying out late on a school night). Instead, he asks what the interests are behind Lee's position.

> **Jim:** Okay, so tell me more about this party and why you want to stay to the end. (Jim is asking about the interests behind Lee's position)
> **Lee explains:** It's a party for Jenna – she's moving back to Madrid at the weekend and this is her leaving party. Everyone is going to be there and I'm going to feel stupid if I have to leave early.
> **Jim:** Okay, so it's an important occasion, and you're going to feel embarrassed if you say your Dad wants you home early. Is that right?

By reflecting back, Jim shows that he *has* listened and tried to understand. He then explains his interests.

> **Jim:** But I'm concerned that what with your weekend job and your studies, considering how unwell you've been recently, going out late tomorrow night as well could set you back with your health.

Having understood each other's position and interests, Jim and Lee then negotiate with each other. Jim agrees to let Lee go to the party if, in return, Lee agrees that instead of walking back from the party – a 45-minute walk – he'll pay for a taxi. Lee also agrees that he'll have some early nights during the rest of the week.

Active Listening

The negotiation process requires that you keep an open mind and be willing to listen to each other's point of view. The other person may have reasons for their position that you find unacceptable, but if you're going to avoid a breakdown in communication or a break in your connection you each need to respect the fact that you have a different but viable opinion about the issue. Respect is important, because without it you won't communicate on an equal footing or take your partner's point of view seriously.

Successful negotiation requires understanding and respecting that the other person's feelings and perspectives may differ from your own. Active listening – reflecting, confirming, and clarifying what the other person has said – not only helps you to see where they're coming from, but also shows that you *are* making an effort to understand things from their perspective.

If you reflect back in this way they are more likely to feel that their point has been heard so there's need to repeat it, defend themselves, or attack your viewpoint.

Reflective listening slows down the exchanges between you. Reflective listening engages a part of the brain – the neocortex – that enables you to think rationally and reasonably. This is just what's needed in a potential conflict situation because it can help stop things escalating too quickly. Reflective listening enables you to understand what the other person is saying and to respond appropriately rather than get involved in a downward-spiralling conversation.

Each person approaches the situation with a position. But staying stuck on those different conflicting positions can stop you from working together towards an agreement. What's crucial is that you each discover the reasons – the interests – behind each other's position. Once you know what's motivating the other person's position, you've got something to negotiate with.

Negotiation is not the same as compromise. In a negotiation, each person gets something in exchange for giving something the other person wants. In compromise, neither person actually gets what they want; they often settle on some middle ground, with the result that neither is satisfied with the solution. Suppose, for example, two people were planning to go to out for dinner and one wanted Turkish food and the other wanted Indian. Their compromise is to go to an Italian restaurant. Although neither person ended up doing something they didn't want to do, neither of them got what they wanted either, so they're less likely to be happy about the result. In a negotiated solution, one partner would pick the restaurant this time and the other the next.

Often, negotiated solutions can work better than compromises because each person gets something they really want in exchange for giving something the other person wants. Each person has an equal say about the situation and so neither feels they haven't been listened to. Furthermore, they also feel like they are giving something to the other person. And that helps them feel good about themselves and the other person. Neither person has 'lost'. It's a win-win situation!

The overriding principle in a negotiated solution is that you get something that meets your needs or interests, and at the same time you give something that meets the other person's needs and interests. If you have something you want from the other person, there's a good chance they want something from you so do think not just about what you want, but what you might be asked and be willing to give in return.

Top Tip

Ask the other person to state what they're prepared to do; what they think is fair and reasonable.

You don't necessarily have to agree and you don't need to let their feelings and opinions dominate yours. You are simply trying to narrow the gap between you both; show that you're willing to try and understand the other person's interests – their point of view, their thoughts and feelings.

***

Top Tip

Listen not just to what is being said, but to what is not being said. Your body language and tone of voice all play a part in being persuasive so try and be aware of your own non-verbal communication. Use open, encouraging body language, not defensive or closed. And when you're asking questions, be sure that your questions don't come across as interrogative, attacking, or defensive.

***

It's important that both of you feel the solution is fair and was arrived at together, that neither of you think that the decision was pushed onto you. Forcing an agreement on one side and reluctantly agreeing or giving in on the other side will not solve the problem. If either person hasn't found the final decision to be completely acceptable, one way or another, the issue is likely to come up again.

A well-negotiated solution – one where you're both genuinely satisfied with the outcome – will mean there's no longer an issue for either of you.

However, if the other person rejects what you're prepared to give, or you're not prepared to give what they want, then what? If this the case, and one of you must give way, then it is fair to negotiate some form of compensation for doing so. But both sides should still feel comfortable with the outcome. So if at work, for example, you were asking for an extra member of staff and your manager resolutely refused then you'd need to fall back on what is known as your BATNA; Best Alternative To a Negotiated Agreement. In this example, that might be a commitment from your manager to increase staff training. Your BATNA is your favoured fallback option if you can't get everything that you want. So when you can, think through in advance what might happen if a negotiation doesn't achieve what you want, and what, for you, might be a good alternative.

In a nutshell

- To persuade people to do something, you'll need to appeal to their heads (logos) and their hearts (pathos). And you'll need to be credible, believable, and trustworthy.
- Avoid trying to persuade someone only according to what issues are important to you, not them. How might they feel about the issue or situation? What do they already know? What are *their* needs, interests, and wants? When might be a good time to talk?
- Don't always assume that you know. Ask questions. What incentives or rewards in return for their cooperation – their time and effort – would they like?
- Very often, persuasion can be most effective if you use suggestion rather than demand.

- If you can tell them how it will benefit them, that's good. But if you can prevent them from losing something, that could be even more persuasive.
- Point out what you think the result or outcome will be of not doing things the way you want, but don't use threats to describe what will happen if they don't do things your way!
- Be clear, confident, and honest about what exactly it is that you want to persuade the other person to do. Keep it focused; simplify your request and don't ramble on.
- Be honest; acknowledge any gain you stand to win. And if you are at risk of losing out, explain what's at stake for you; what you're concerned about.
- Say what you're prepared to do towards it. People are more likely to help do something rather than do the whole thing.
- Listen to the response. People are more likely to cooperate if they feel acknowledged and understood. Are you clear about their concerns and objections? Acknowledge and address those objections.
- Listening with an open mind means being willing to listen to someone else's experience, their opinions and ideas, without making assumptions or jumping to conclusions.
- You may disagree, but because you listened, you know exactly what it is you are disagreeing

with. And you might learn something useful or interesting.

- Arguing against someone else's way of seeing or doing things can result in what's known as 'the backfire effect'. It can cause them to find reasons to support their original stance more strongly than they previously did.
- Think about the counterargument. It may seem counterintuitive, but you'll be more persuasive if you acknowledge and address the opposing point of view.
- With a steel-manning approach, you acknowledge that what the other person said is valid and understandable. You then explain how what you're saying logically leads on from what they're saying.
- Use positive language. Your aim is to be understood and get someone to see or do things your way. Positive words and phrases make that more likely to happen.
- There's a difference between positions and interests. Your position is where you stand on an issue; your point of view. Your interests are the reasons why you think and feel that way; what's important or is of concern.
- What's crucial is that you each discover the reasons – the interests – behind each other's position. Once you know what's motivating the other person's position, you've got something to negotiate with.

- Negotiation is not the same as compromise. In a negotiation, each person gets something in exchange for giving something the other person wants. In compromise, neither person actually gets what they want; they often settle on some middle ground, with the result that neither is satisfied with the solution.
- The key principle in a negotiated solution is that you *both* get something that meets your needs or interests. Each person has an equal say, each person is listened to, each person knows they are giving something to the other person.
- When you can, think through in advance what might happen if a negotiation doesn't achieve what you want, and what, for you, might be a good alternative.

About the Author

Gill Hasson is a teacher, trainer, and writer. She has 20 years' experience in the area of personal development. Her expertise is in the areas of confidence and self-esteem, communication skills, assertiveness, and resilience.

Gill delivers teaching and training for educational organizations, voluntary and business organizations, and the public sector.

Gill is the author of the bestselling *Mindfulness* and *Emotional Intelligence* plus other books on the subjects of dealing with difficult people, resilience, communication skills, and assertiveness.

Gill's particular interest and motivation is in helping people to realize their potential, to live their best life! You can contact Gill via her website www.gillhasson.co.uk or email her at gillhasson@btinternet.com.

Other Books by Gill Hasson

Mindfulness: Be Mindful. Live in the Moment

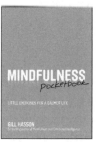

Mindfulness Pocketbook: Little Exercises for a Calmer Life

The Mindfulness Colouring and Activity Book: Calming Colouring and De-stressing Doodles to Focus Your Busy Mind

Emotional Intelligence – Managing Emotions to Make a Positive Impact on your Life and Career

Emotional Intelligence Pocketbook: Little Exercises for an Intuitive Life

Confidence Pocketbook: Little Exercises for a Self-Assured Life

Positive Thinking: Find Happiness and Achieve Your Goals Through the Power of Positive Thought

How to Deal with Difficult People: Smart Tactics for Overcoming the Problem People in your Life

Declutter Your Life: How Outer Order Leads to Inner Calm

Happiness: How to Get into the Habit of Being Happy

Kindness: Change Your Life and Make the World a Kinder Place

Overcoming Anxiety: Reassuring Ways to Break Free from Stress and Worry and Lead a Calmer Life

Positive Thinking Pocketbook: Little Exercises for a Happy and Successful Life

Productivity: Get Motivated, get Organised and Get Things Done

Index

Index